D0180949

BACKCOUNTRY
MEDICAL
GUIDE

By the same author

Two and Two Halves to Bhutan (1970)
Doctor on Everest (1972)
Atlin's Gold (1995)
Eric Shipton: Everest and Beyond (1998)

Wilderness Medical Society (US) Handbook
(co-author) (1998)

BACKCOUNTRY MEDICAL GUIDE

SECOND EDITION

PETER STEELE, M.D.

THE
MOUNTAINEERS

Published by
The Mountaineers
1001 SW Klickitat Way, Suite 201
Seattle, WA 98134

© 1988, 1999 by Peter Steele

Originally published in Great Britain by Constable and Company Limited under the title *Medical Handbook for Walkers and Climbers*.

Published in North America by The Mountaineers.

Manufactured in the United States of America

Cover design by Helen Cherullo
Cover photograph: *Climbers Approaching Aconcagua, Horcones Valley* © Scott Darsney

Library of Congress Cataloging-in-Publication Data available

 Printed on recycled paper

To Eric Langmuir

CONTENTS

Contents

LIST OF DIAGRAMS

(drawings by Rodney Paull)

ACKNOWLEDGEMENTS

In previous editions of this book I relied on many experts who have sealed it with authority and helped ensure its accuracy. My debt to them is immense. This revision was vetted thoroughly by Barney Rosedale, Everester, erstwhile physician in rural Nepal and wise family doctor. Any errors or omissions are my own and I would appreciate hearing of them.

PS

PREFACE

The aim of this book is to help walkers and climbers on the hills to muster their wits during the first few shattering minutes after an accident or a medical emergency in order to keep the victim alive and prevent any worsening before reaching skilled care.

A recurring question of helpful critics has been, 'Who is your audience?' The book is for anyone who ventures into mountains or wilderness – a teacher leading schoolchildren on a hike over Snowdon, a maestro mountaineer on the Brenva Face in the Alps, or a young doctor trekking in the Arun Valley of the Himalaya. Your medical knowledge will vary widely, and yet I have written one book for everyone in hope of interesting you all – a dangerous task open to much criticism.

I struggled with the question of how to refer to the injured party – victim, climber, casualty, patient, trekker, person – and settled on a mixture of whatever sounded most comfortable in the text. I ask indulgence of female readers because I generally refer to the masculine gender solely for ease of syntax.

Economy of words, plain English and clear meaning are my paramount aim throughout. Jargon bedevils my profession and is a cloak of mystique under which doctors can hide. When a medical word is apt I am not shy to use it.

To separate common information from more technical detail, and to avoid burdening the average person with gobbledegook, matters of interest to the more medically trained reader, or those superfluous to immediate practical help, appear in small print.

INTRODUCTION

Accidents and medical crises create anxiety and tension. When ambulance sirens wail and strobe lights flash adrenalin courses through the veins of experienced emergency physicians as they wonder what horror will unfold when the ambulance doors open. In the mountains you may be far from help with few resources and meagre medical knowledge, a situation that readily causes panic and confusion unless you, the rescuer, keep a cool head and act decisively.

Assess the person's condition and decide what needs doing immediately to prevent him worsening or dying before you can get help. Unless you marshal your thoughts clearly and quickly during this lonely, anxious time you may flounder.

This is where I hope this book will help; but you should have read it at least once at home before throwing it in the bottom of your pack – where I hope it will stay while you are out on the hills.

Accident prevention

Prevention, if enacted, would make this book redundant; but in an imperfect world prevention, sadly, will never be complete. Mountains are hazardous, and some people will get hurt, and may die, whatever help you may give them. Only a thorough apprenticeship will hone your technical skills and turn you into a well-rounded mountaineer able to handle these dangers. Learn everything possible about the wilderness before venturing into it, apply commonsense while there, and judge when to accept defeat and turn back rather than press on towards disaster.

Medical problems on mountains are often problems of mountains more than of medicine. To splint a broken leg and treat the pain is comparatively easy, but how to evacuate a victim safely without further injury, illness, or hypothermia will depend on your hard-won skill and experience. A big medical kit and all the newest gear will not lessen the dangers. Carry only essentials because, if weighed down by impedimenta, you will expend precious energy needed for coping with the unexpected.

A well-trained first-aider may be more useful in the wilderness than a doctor who is ignorant of the special problems of remote places. An MB (or whatever) after his name does not necessarily mean he is any better than a competent outdoorsman who has learned the basic medical skills. Nature cures more often than any doctor.

The law

Good Samaritans in the outdoors are unlikely to fall foul of the law when their attempts to save life fail, provided they apply conscientiously skills learned and stay within their capabilities. In legal parlance the word 'reasonable' occurs repeatedly. But nothing will protect you from your own gross negligence or unwarranted interference. Although expected to give reasonable help within the limits of your experience, do not jeopardise your own safety. However, once you have started treating a victim you are bound to continue until more skilled help is available. Legal action looms large these days, so the lily-livered should stay well away from rescuing. Like adventure, it carries risks but we still attempt both.

1

ASSESSING THE VICTIM

The accident scene

After an accident one single person should take charge in order to prevent confusion from too many people offering smart ideas. If reticent to lead, give your support to a leader who has first-aid experience, and thereby influence the operation from the sidelines.

Plan a safe approach to the casualty. In mountains, for example, come from below or from the side, but not from above where a rock-slide or an avalanche may start. If possible, move the victim to safe level ground, make a shelter and keep him warm. Undo tight clothing and equipment, cutting along seams if necessary. Do the minimum first-aid on site to stabilize him until you can reach skilled medical help, which may yet be far away. Panicking bystanders put pressure on a first-aider to *do* something, but knowing what *not to do* is more important. Action for action's sake may lead to meddlesome interference. Whatever you may do, not-so-bad accident victims tend to get better, while very bad ones tend to get worse and die.

Care

Care must be total care of the whole person – frightened, anxious, and in pain – not just bandaging his wounds. First, comfort him, especially if it appears he may die. Compassion needs no medical skill, just warm caring humanity. Call him by name; tell him your name, who you are, and your first-aid qualifications. Touching forges a bond of trust; hold his hand or lay your hand on his shoulder.

Make him as comfortable as the ground allows; let him pee if he wishes. While waiting for, and during, the rescue, insulate him from the cold ground below; this is more important than piling clothes on top to keep him warm. An immobile injured person can quickly become hypothermic, and this may be more lethal than his injury.

Moving him may cause pain, so give ample warning to avoid surprise. Withhold pain-killers, usually until after examining him so as not to disguise pain and obscure physical signs; but if pain is severe, treat it regardless.

Examine him carefully and thoroughly to lessen the chance of missing some important sign, but also to bolster his confidence by reassuring him your care will be thorough. Then explain fully his situation, telling no lies. He will be anxious about being crippled, that his job will be jeopardized, what his family will say. He may feel guilty at being the cause of so much trouble; blaming him is pointless even if the accident was his fault. From now on he will be totally dependent on your rescue skills and such dependence erodes self-esteem. Encourage him to discuss the accident and dispel his guilt and embarrassment. Listen without judging.

Make a plan of action, discuss it with the victim, and try to involve him in his own rescue. He may be able to hold a rope, or light a stove to boil water for tea while you attend to other things.

Assessment

A quick but careful scrutiny of the victim should reveal the main injuries or problems; a full and leisurely exam can follow once this most urgent question has been answered:

Is he or she in immediate danger of dying?

A person injured in the mountains is most likely to die from:
– extensive damage to the entire body caused by the accident
– inability to breathe owing to airway block or chest injury
– severe head injury and the sequels of unconsciousness
– profuse bleeding causing shock and heart stop.

Act before trying to identify the precise cause of trouble in any of the above conditions, provided not patently hopeless. In other cases there is usually sufficient time to ask the person what happened, and examine him thoroughly to assemble the facts that will contribute to a reasoned diagnosis. Doctors and medical personnel are trained this way and other people should do the same. (Some medical terms used in the following section may be unclear unless you have read the relevant chapters in this book.)

Initial survey

The scheme: *Ask, Look, Listen, Feel, Move, Act, Treat,* is a rough framework for most of the chapters in this book. Pithy words and explicit phrases in plain English are preferable to verbose jargon e.g. examination, observation, auscultation, palpation.

Airway:
listen for the snoring breathing of airway block. Tilt the person's head, lift the jaw, and turn him into the draining position. Remove secretions and insert an oral airway. Do not pillow the head.

Breathing:
listen for normal quiet breathing or obstructed croaking stridor; look for rise and fall of the lower chest and upper abdomen. If absent, start rescue breathing (see page 57).

Circulation:
look for blood from an exposed wound; feel under the head
and back for pooled blood soaked in clothing. Look at the
face for the pallor of shock and the blue tinge of cyanosis.
Feel the pulse at the wrist or neck, and notice the speed of
return of colour to a pressure-blanched nailbed, to assess
the circulation. Control bleeding with steady pressure
directly on the wound.

Neurological:
assess the conscious level by simple questioning or response
to pain. Look at the pupils; a difference in size may indicate
bleeding inside the skull. Look at the nose and ears for
cerebro-spinal fluid leaking from a fracture at the base of
the skull.

Bones:
feel the skull, chest and pelvis for fractures, and move the
limbs gently, watching the person's face for painful wincing.
If possible, restore natural alignment by reducing dislocations and splinting fractures.

Full examination

Make sure the victim is not in urgent need of life-saving
attention, and if necessary move him to a safe place out of
danger of rockfall or avalanche and with space to move
around. Then do a thorough and leisurely exam.

ASK
Ask a conscious person for a full story of the accident or
illness, and of any symptoms (the feelings of which he complains); if unconscious, ask a witness. Follow a similar routine every time you ask a history and examine someone;

thereby, as in a pilot's pre-flight check, you will miss nothing important. Always write down findings immediately because you may forget details later. An accurate written record will assist the receiving hospital doctor. Whatever scheme you adopt, stick to it so it becomes routine.

General questions
– name, age, address, next of kin, occupation
– chief complaint; use the person's own words to write a sequential story of the accident or illness. Ask specially about pain: time of onset, nature, severity, change in character
– past illnesses and surgery, with dates
– present medical problems and current medication; look for a Medic-Alert bracelet or medallion
– allergies to drugs, foods, and insect stings
– last intake by mouth.

Systematic history
– heart: chest pain, palpitations, shortness of breath, swelling of ankles

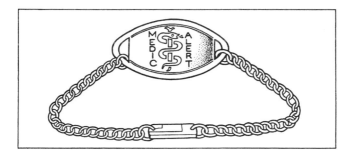

Medic-Alert bracelet

- chest: cough and sputum, difficult breathing, wheeze or croup
- gut: pain, appetite, nausea, vomiting, indigestion, constipation or diarrhoea
- urine: frequency, pain, burning, volume and colour
- nerves: conscious level; seizures, faints, headaches; loss of power or sensation, numbness or tingling
- motor: pain or weakness in bones, muscles or joints; abnormal gait and walking.

Examine
the person under shelter, with adequate light, and undressed so nothing is obscured by clothing; remember the back as well as the front. Cold hands will make him flinch and you will learn nothing. The order in which you examine the person and how you record the findings is unimportant so long as your scheme is unvarying. Start at the crown of the head and work towards the feet. When examining a paired part, e.g. a limb or one side of the chest, always expose the opposite side; slight swelling or deformity becomes obvious when compared with the normal side. Record negative findings which may be as important as positive ones. Perform every step of the exam, even if the injury or illness appears obvious at first sight, because a secondary condition obscured by an urgent chief complaint may be equally significant. Reassess the person frequently (at least every half hour), because much can change after the initial exam.

The following outline is a rough check-list; refer to specific chapters for detail. Examining someone requires practice and skill, but all doctors were once inept medical students. This scheme presupposes no specialized medical equipment.

General appearance
- sick or well (an impression formed by instinct rather than by specific signs)
- response; conscious level and degree of co-operation

- demeanour (lying still, rolling around)
- pain, temperature, fever
- skin colour: anaemia (pink or pale lower inner eyelids or finger-nails), cyanosis (blue inside lips), jaundice (yellow eyeballs)
- skin eruptions
- hands: tell a whole story about the person.

Head and neck
- scalp: bleeding, swelling, depressions
- eyes: vision, pupil size, redness, pussy discharge
- ears: hearing, discharge (blood or clear fluid)
- nose: airway, bleeding, discharge
- mouth: bleeding, breath smell, teeth and gums, tongue, jaw
- throat: redness, ulceration, pus
- glands: neck, below jaw.

Heart
- pulse rate and regularity
- blood pressure (judged by the force of the pulse and speed of the nail bed's return to a pink colour after blanching with pressure)
- peripheral circulation (warmth and colour of the fingers and toes)
- ankle swelling and pitting on pressure
- heart sounds (ear to chest) – but difficult to interpret for non-medical rescuers).

Chest
- visible injury (bruising or fracture)
- breathing movements and sounds (ear to chest for air entry, wheeze and fluid, crackling or bubbling).

Abdomen
- quiet movement on breathing

- scars from previous surgery, distension, swellings
- tenderness, resistance to the examining hand, rigidity of muscle wall, masses or swellings, hernial openings, genitals.

Pelvis and perineum
- stability and pain on pressing firmly on hips
- bruising between legs
- bleeding from urinary passage.

Muscles and joints
- (for all limbs and joints) range of movement, pain, tenderness, swelling, deformity, power, tone, co-ordination, sensation, reflexes.

Neurological
- conscious level and mental state
- pupil size and reaction to light.

2

EQUIPMENT AND DRUGS

Before setting out on a journey to drive across the Sahara or sail the Pacific it is wise to check the tool kit (and the machine or craft) in case of a breakdown. For similar reasons the section on equipment and drugs is included at the very start of this book so the reader may know what is available for dealing with an emergency.

The first-aid and medical kit should fit in a sealed waterproof plastic box. An expedition will need bulkier equipment and more drugs to stock base camp, especially if a doctor who knows how to use them is present. The equipment and drugs below are intended only to be a check-list from which you can make up your own kit to fit the box of your choice – and your own expertise.

Swiss army knife = SAK   Leatherman knife = LM.

First-aid kit

soap bar
alcohol antiseptic swabs
bandage strips (assorted)
Elastoplast strip 3"
surgical tape 1"
duct tape 3"
Steri-strips
moleskin
Super Glue

bandage: elastic 3"
      crepe 3"
      triangular
safety pins
gauze: sterile plain
      non-stick
wound dressing
  (compressed pads)

tulle gras: paraffin
  antibiotic-impregnated
gelatin foam
scalpel blade #15
tweezers (SAK)
scissors (SAK)
matches, waterproof
luggage label & wax pencil

notebook &
  soft waterproof pencil
magnifying glass
  (inverted camera lens)
tongue depressor
penlight
thermometer, regular
oral airway

Medical box

all of the First-aid kit
  plus:
flashlight
thermometer, low reading
antiseptic concentrate
tincture of benzoin
finger dressing, Tubegauz
head dressing, elastic
  net
forceps, thumb
forceps, locking

syringes: 3ml & 10ml
       20ml +
       flexible catheter
       tip (for irrigation)
needles, hypodermic
  #20 & #25
needle holder (LM)
sutures: 2/0 catgut
      4/0 nylon
surgical gloves
stethoscope

Base camp equipment

all of the First-aid kit and
Medical box plus:
blood pressure machine
ophthalmoscope
auroscope
plaster of Paris/fibreglass
tape
wire mesh splints
neck collar
Foley catheter

i/v drip set
i/v fluids
nasopharyngeal airway
cricothyrotomy tube
(sterile, wrapped)
dental forceps: upper
              lower
dental probe

Drugs

D.1 Analgesics

D.1.1 paracetamol	500mg tab
D.1.2 ibuprofen	400mg tab
D.1.3 codeine	15mg tab
D.1.4 morphine	15mg tab (+ 15mg/ml amp)
D.1.5 naloxone	20mcg/ml amp

D.2 Antibiotics

D.2.1 cephalosporin	250mg tab (+ amp)
D.2.2 co-trimoxazole	960mg tab
D.2.3 metronidazole	250mg tab (+ suppos)

D.3 Antihistamines

D.3.1 promethazine	25mg tab (+ 25mg/ml amp)
D.3.2 chlorpheniramine	4mg tab

D.4 Steroids

D.4.1 prednisone	5mg tab
D.4.2 dexamethasone	0.5mg tab (+ 5mg/ml amp)

D.5 Sedatives

D.5.1 lorazepam	1mg tab

D.6 Diuretics

D.6.1 frusemide	40mg tab (+ 10mg/ml amp)
D.6.2 acetazolamide	250mg tab

D.7 Cardio-vascular drugs

D.7.1 glyceryl trinitrate	0.5mg tab
D.7.2 adrenaline	1 mg/ml inj

D.8 Respiratory drugs

D.8.1 salbutamol	4mg tab (+ puffer)

D.9 Digestive system drugs

D.9.1 aluminium hydroxide	500mg tab
D.9.2 cimetidine	400mg tab
D.9.3 loperamide	2mg tab
D.9.4 bisacodyl	5mg tab
D.9.5 bismuth subgallate	200mg suppos

D.10 Skin antiseptics

D.10.1 povidone iodine	concentrate

D.11 Skin applications

D.11.1 betamethasone	0.1% oint
D.11.2 clotrimazole	1% cream
D.11.3 PABA sunscreen	
D.11.4 calamine	
D.11.5 lip salve	
D.11.6 methyl salicylate	oint

D.12 Eyes

D.12.1 chloramphenicol	1% oint
D.12.2 dexamethasone	0.1% oint
D.12.3 homatropine	2% drops
D.12.4 local anaesthetic	drops

D.13 Ears

D.13.1 chloramphenicol	1% oint

D.14 Nose

D.14.1 phenylephrine	2.5% drops

D.15 Throat

D.15.1 lozenges	

D.16 Teeth

D.16.1 oil of cloves	
D.16.2 temporary filling	

D.17 Local anaesthetic
D.17.1 xylocaine 2%   20mg/ml vial

D.18 Oral rehydration constituents (see page 43)

D.19 Water purification
D.19.1 iodine tabs
D.19.2 chlorine tabs

Myths extol the merits of particular drugs, encouraged by
the habits of prescribers and by advertising propaganda of
drug manufacturers. Certain principles in recommending
drugs are explained here; base your choice on fact and good
advice.

In the text I use the scientific, generic names of drugs by
which they are known world-wide. Prescribing by the generic name is usually cheaper because drug companies load
the cost of research and development onto their own brand
names. It is also safer by avoiding confusion over the name,
which is the same in Tokyo or Timbuktu. When two drugs
have similar action I choose the cheaper; although cost is a
factor in assembling a good medical kit it should not ham-
string the choice if an expensive drug is preferable. We are
dealing in small quantities and, when needed, only the best
drug will do. Drugs with more than one action are preferred.
To avoid confusing a harassed rescuer I have selected one
tried and tested drug, or possibly two, from each treatment
category rather than offering you several choices; e.g. dozens
of different antihistamines are available but promethazine
and chlorpheniramine have stood the test of time. Taking
medication once or twice daily is most easily remembered.

When recommending a drug or a piece of equipment I
avoid writing repeatedly 'if available'. Included in my selec-
tion are such drugs and medical material as might reasonably be included in a mountain medical kit, which should
be comprehensive, compact and light. Most drugs are

conveniently carried as pills or tablets rather than as liquids, which freeze, are bulky, and the bottles or ampoules break easily. However, some drugs preferably are injected for speed of action, control, and to avoid vomiting; this book presumes that medical boxes may include them (and they will necessarily require syringes and needles as well) or that they may be found at base camp. The technique of intramuscular injection can be learned easily, and practised on an orange, which has the form and consistence of skin. Intravenous injection requires more skill, but millions of junkies know how.

The drugs chosen cover the widest spectrum of action; e.g. antibiotics cephalosporin and co-trimoxazole cover a wide range of bacterial possibilities with few side-effects. If the person is sensitive to one, use the other. Sound hospital medicine is quite different to that practicable in the wilderness with a small medical kit and limited experience, so you may have to choose drugs that a city doctor would shun. Doses apply to an average-sized adult. Adjust dosage for size and age; children take roughly half the adult dose, infants a quarter. The possible major side-effects of the drugs are spelled out. Pregnant women should beware of taking any drugs unless medically advised.

Morphine and codeine are controlled drugs, only prescribable by a registered physician under specific guidelines. When approached by explorers for small quantities of such drugs for their first-aid kits or medical boxes, provided I know the person is competent to use the drugs safely, I prescribe a small amount (30 tablets maximum), writing the name of the person followed in red ink by 'for expedition use only'. I instruct him to write down each time the name of the victim to whom he administers the drugs, the date, and the quantity; he must produce this before I will re-prescribe. This seems a reasonable way to observe the law regarding controlled drugs, although little specific is written concerning non-medical people dispensing such drugs.

Each drug (D) has a number; the first figure refers to the category, the second to its place within that group, for example (D.1.3) means the drug is in category 1, analgesics, and is number 3, codeine. In the text I refer to this number, and the rescuer must refer back to this chapter for details of action, dosage, and side-effects. When the choice is equal I just give the category number (D.1).

The specialized drugs and chemicals mentioned in chapter 22 exist only there, not in this general drugs section. When in the text I recommend a drug that does not appear in the medical box, it is bracketed thus [ergometrine].

Certain standard abbreviations occur throughout the book:

s/e – side-effects	g – grams
i/m – intramuscular	mg – milligrams
i/v – intravenous	mcg – micrograms
s/l – sublingual	l – litres
s/c – subcutaneous	ml – millilitres
	tsp – teaspoon
	tbsp – tablespoon

This chapter warrants careful study before reading the rest of the text.

D.1 PAIN RELIEF – analgesics

Pain is always unpleasant and often unnecessary because, with adequate dosage of analgesics, most pain can be controlled. Peoples' stoicism varies as does their response to analgesics.

MILD ANALGESICS

Paracetamol will control most headache and mild muscular or skeletal pain, and reduce fever. It has little anti-inflammatory action. It causes less irritation to, and bleeding from, the stomach than aspirin, and fewer sensitivity reactions. Use aspirin only in its enteric-coated forms which diminish the acid corrosive effects on the stomach.

Ibuprofen, one of many anti-inflammatory drugs unrelated to steroids, is also analgesic and may be taken in addition to other stronger narcotic analgesics. It is useful for inflammatory conditions like arthritis, tendonitis, and bursitis.

Compound analgesics containing aspirin or paracetamol mixed with codeine or caffeine or both, have no advantages and are expensive.

D.1.1 paracetamol

Treat: 500mg–1g every 4 to 6 hours to maximum 4g daily

s/e: rare hypersensitivity and skin rashes

D.1.2 ibuprofen

Treat: 400mg 3 or 4 times daily

s/e: occasional stomach upset – so take with food, and use cautiously with sufferers of stomach ulcers, asthma, and aspirin sensitivity; it may cause fluid retention at altitude.

MODERATE ANALGESICS

Codeine relieves moderate pain, and together with paracetamol boosts the analgesic effect. It suppresses cough, and reduces bowel motility to slow diarrhoea. It is the analgesic of choice in head injury because pupil size and breathing are affected less than by morphine. Codeine is legally narcotic and potentially addictive, but dependency is uncommon.

D.1.3 codeine phosphate

Treat: 10–60mg by mouth every 4 hours to a maximum 400mg daily

s/e: constipation, drowsiness, dizziness, alcohol enhancement.

STRONG ANALGESICS

Morphine is a time-honoured strong analgesic effective against severe pain. It is narcotic, causing sleepiness, creates euphoria and is also strongly addictive. Because it depresses breathing do not use it when breathing is compromised, as in head injury, some chest injuries, asthma, and at high altitude. In head injury it also alters pupil size, an important diagnostic sign. Pain relief from morphine is dose-related, as are its unwanted effects. It constipates; it may cause nausea and vomiting, that can be lessened if combined with promethazine which may even enhance the analgesic power.

Swallowed morphine tablets are absorbed poorly from the stomach and the drug is broken down by the liver before it reaches its site of action in the brain. The newer synthetic opioid buprenorphine (Temgesic), placed under the tongue, although bitter-tasting, is an alternative. Morphine is true and tried and has traditionally been given i/v in small doses, repeated as often as needed. If given i/m to a shocked person the injected drug can lie stagnant in the muscle; when blood pressure and circulation pick up, suddenly a slug of drug is released with the danger of profoundly depressing breathing. Ideally, keep the narcotic antagonist drug naloxone handy to reverse respiratory depression.

Pethidine is weaker than morphine and has no advantages, so gets no space here.

D.1.4 morphine sulphate

Treat: 10–30mg maximum every 4 hours s/l, s/c, or i/m (slow release preparation preferable)

5mg i/v every 5 minutes until pain eases and then repeated as frequently as needed to control pain

s/e: respiratory depression, constipation, urinary retention, nausea, tolerance and dependance. Avoid in head injury, chest injury, asthma, breathing difficulty, at high altitude, and with druggies

D.1.5 naloxone, narcotic antagonist

Treat: 40–200mcg i/v, and add 40 mcg every 2 minutes as needed to restore normal breathing; it can also be given i/m or s/c

s/e: nausea and vomiting.

D.2 ANTIBIOTICS

Antibiotic drugs combat bacterial infections; virus illnesses are generally untreatable so eschew antibiotics. Ideally, bacteria should be grown in culture and their sensitivity ascertained before starting an appropriate antibiotic. However, in wilderness scientific accuracy is impossible and a blunderbuss approach is in order, using an educated guess at which broad-spectrum antibiotic will be effective.

The only logical way to choose amongst the myriad antibiotics on the market is to take sound bacteriological advice and select two or three antibiotics to combat the widest range of organisms, allowing for cost and availability. Cephalosphorins have superceded amoxycillin (a broad-spectrum penicillin which used to be the antibiotic of choice) because many organisms have become resistant to it. 5% of the population are penicillin-sensitive, but only 10% of penicillin-sensitive people are allergic to cephalosporins. 90% of Staphylococcus aureus, the universal organism of wound and soft tissue infections, and burns (all of which may be commonly encountered in wilderness) are resistant to amoxycillin whereas cephalospirins are usually effective.

Cephalosporin is the name of a group of broad-spectrum antibiotics of which there are several to choose from, all with similar actions. Hence the group name rather than any single drug – but take advice from a doctor or pharmacist. Cephalosporins are very effective given i/v.

Cephalosporins are *bactericidal* and combat Group A streptococci, most strains of Staphylococcus aureus, Escherichia coli, Proteus mirabilis, Klebsiella pneumoniae, and Strep. pneumoniae – but are ineffective against pseudomonas and Strep. (Enterococcus) faecalis.

Treat: against infections of skin and soft tissue, the middle ear, upper and lower respiratory tract (including streptococcal sore throat), and urinary tract.

Co-trimoxazole, a mixture of 5 parts sulphamethoxazole and 1 part trimethoprim, is the other antibiotic of choice.

Co-trimoxazole is *bacteriostatic* and effective against many strains of Staph. aureus, H. influenzae, Strep. pneumoniae, E. coli, Klebsiella, Enterobacter, Proteus mirabilis, Salmonella typhi and paratyphi, and shigella – but ineffective against Strep. faecalis and Group A streptococci.

Treat: against infections of burns, skin and soft tissue, bone and joints, the lower respiratory tract (bronchitis and pneumonia), and urinary tract; it is useful for bacterial diarrhoea and in people who are allergic to penicillins and cephalosporins, though not if they are sulpha-sensitive. A known doubly-sensitive person on a trip should take [doxycycline] or [erythromycin] as a substitute.

Metronidazole (Flagyl) is active against anaerobic bacteria and protozoa, but has less antibacterial value than either cephalosporin or co-trimoxazole. It is well absorbed, giving high blood levels for a prolonged period. In the wilds far from help it would cope with persistent diarrhoea of Entameba histolytica or Giardia lamblia, and appendicitis, especially with peritonitis following a ruptured appendix.

A full course of antibiotics usually lasts 5 to 7 days so do not curtail it, but lengthen it if the response is slow. For convenience antibiotics are usually taken by mouth but in severe infections they are more effective i/v, though only sophisticated medical kits will carry them in this form. Avoid alcohol with antibiotics.

D.2.1 cephalosporin

Treat: dose and frequency vary, so seek medical advice for your particular choice. Double the dose in severe infection

s/e: hypersensitivity and allergic symptoms of urticaria,

rashes, nausea, vomiting, diarrhoea, and in rare cases, anaphylaxis

D.2.2 co-trimoxazole

Treat: 1 double-strength (DS) tablet twice daily, doubled
in severe infection

s/e: nausea, vomiting, rashes, and various blood disorders

D.2.3 metronidazole

Treat: 500mg every 8–12 hours

s/e: nausea, drowsiness, headache, rashes.

D.3 ANTIHISTAMINES

Antihistamines dampen allergic reactions and ease hay
fever, itching, skin rashes, vertigo and motion sickness; they
are mildly hypnotic. They are used i/v in emergency treatment of severe allergic reactions but are of no value in
asthma.

Promethazine alleviates nausea and vomiting, lasts up to
12 hours, but is quite soporific; it can be given together with
morphine, the analgesic effect of which is not diminished
and may even be enhanced.

Chlorpheniramine is shorter-acting, and causes less drowsiness, so is good for daytime use in treating allergies.

D.3.1 promethazine (Phenergan)

Treat: 25mg by mouth every 8 hours to maximum 150mg
daily

s/e: drowsiness, headaches, urinary retention, dry mouth,
blurred vision

D.3.2 chlorpheniramine

Treat: 4mg by mouth every 8 hours

s/e: less sedating than other antihistamines.

D.4 STEROIDS

Dexamethasone (a powerful relative of prednisone) causes
widespread effects on the body, so requires caution. It suppresses severe allergic reactions and may be effective in
severe asthma, status asthmaticus, and acute hypersensi-

tivity reactions like food and drug allergy and insect stings. In the wilds its powerful anti-inflammatory action could save the day for someone with an acute prolapsed disc or a severe gout attack by allowing them to walk to safety. It may reduce brain swelling in cerebral oedema of high altitude, and in trauma from head injury.

People taking steroids should wear a Medic-Alert bracelet or medallion, and carry a card in their wallet with instructions on how to adjust their dose in case of emergency.

D.4.1 dexamethasone (Decadron)
Treat: 4mg i/m or by mouth every 4 to 6 hours, or 10mg i/v, or i/m. Reduce steroids gradually, but you can stop them abruptly if taken for less than 3 weeks.

s/e: steroids have many hazards, particularly in suppressing adrenal gland function and the normal inflammatory response, so they require medical supervision.

D.5 SEDATIVES
Benzodiazepines are useful hypnotics for insomnia (e.g. for long plane flights) and as sedatives in low doses for acute anxiety. When given i/v they may control epileptic seizures until the person can begin specific anti-epileptic medication. Benzodiazepines differ mainly in their length of action. *Lorazepam* is one of many available, being fairly quick of onset, short in action, and less cumulative than other benzodiazepines.

Promethazine (D.3.1) is a useful mild sedative.

D.5.1 lorazepam
Treat: 1 to 2mg at night, 0.5 to 1mg by day
s/e: drowsiness, dependency, habituation.

D.6 DIURETICS
Diuretics promote urine flow and decrease oedema (the abnormal accumulation of body fluids) by suppressing reabsorption of sodium by the kidney; coincidentally they lower blood pressure.

Frusemide is powerful and short-acting; use with caution, only the smallest dose to get the required effect. It can treat oedema of heart failure, and peripheral oedema of the feet, ankles, and hands. Diuresis (peeing) starts within 1 hour and is complete in 6 hours, so take it in the morning to avoid disturbing sleep. Used over a long time, frusemide causes loss of potassium, which must be replaced by potassium tablets or by fruit juice.

Acetazolamide can prevent and treat acute mountain sickness (AMS) (see page 244) but is never a substitute for descent.

D.6.1 frusemide (Lasix)

Treat: 40 to 120mg daily by mouth, i/v not faster than 4mg/minute

s/e: potassium loss, dehydration, rashes, ringing in the ears

D.6.2 acetazolamide (Diamox)

Treat: 250mg twice daily (forbidden for people allergic to sulpha drugs)

s/e: numbness and tingling of fingers, toes, face; dry mouth, makes beer taste foul.

D.7 CARDIO-VASCULAR DRUGS

People with heart problems usually carry their own medications; the wilderness is no place to start cardiac drugs of unpredictable action and patient response.

Glyceryl trinitrate dilates blood vessels to the heart and relieves the chest pain of angina; it works within seconds and lasts less than 1 hour.

Adrenaline relieves acute asthma, severe allergic reactions and anaphylactic shock; in older people it can cause an irregular heartbeat.

Digoxin is risky to use, so is excluded from a medical kit.

D.7.1 glyceryl trinitrate

Treat: 0.5 to 1mg under the tongue and repeat in ½ hour if needed

s/e: throbbing headache, flushing, faintness

D.7.2 adrenaline

Treat: 0.5 to 1mg of 1:1000 solution s/c every 10 to 15 minutes for 3 doses (if needed)

s/e: rapid, irregular pulse, anxiety, tremor, dry mouth, cold hands and feet.

D.8 RESPIRATORY DRUGS

Salbutamol is a safe bronchodilator that relaxes the tight wheezy breathing of asthma; inhaled from an aerosol puffer it works rapidly; when taken by mouth it is more sustained but has more side-effects. Beware of using the puffer too often because the drug is unevenly absorbed.

D.8.1 salbutamol (Ventolin)

Treat: 4mg by mouth every 6 to 8 hours; 2 puffs of aerosol every 6 to 8 hours; 0.25 to 0.5mg s/c or i/v in severe asthma

s/e: rapid pulse, headache, tremor.

D.9 DIGESTIVE SYSTEM DRUGS

Antacids neutralize acid produced by the stomach and, taken frequently after meals, ease the discomfort of indigestion, gastritis, and the pain of peptic ulcer. Roll packets are convenient to carry in the pocket; crush and chew to paste for greater effect. Along with medication, eliminate fatty or spiced foods, and avoid nicotine, alcohol and coffee, all of which encourage gastric acid secretion.

D.9.1 aluminium hydroxide

Treat: 500mg tablets as needed.

Acid-reducing drugs block histamine receptors in the stomach, reduce gastric acid, and allow healing of peptic ulcers, but have no effect once they bleed.

D.9.2 cimetidine

Treat: 400mg twice daily

s/e: diarrhoea, skin rashes, dizziness.

Gut-slowing drugs reduce the motility of the gut and ease diarrhoea, as do all narcotic drugs (an undesirable effect when used for pain relief).

Loperamide is poorly absorbed from the gut so remains there longer where its action is needed; use together with codeine (D.1.3) for greatest effect. Antibiotics should generally be avoided in diarrhoea, which may be worsened because they kill normal and necessary bowel organisms as well as harmful ones.

D.9.3 loperamide (Imodium)

Treat: 2mg every 8 hours

s/e: dry mouth, rashes

Laxatives of natural dietary roughage and fibre, e.g. horses' bran and whole wheat, along with fruit juice, especially of prune or fig, are simpler and safer than drugs.

Gentle purgatives or motility-increasing drugs stimulate gut motility within 6 to 12 hours.

D.9.4 bisacodyl (Dulcolax)

Treat: 5 to 10mg by mouth after meals; by suppository 10mg

s/e: abdominal cramps, diarrhoea

Piles and anal itching ease with scrupulous toilet: wash with soap and water after a bowel movement, avoid constipation, and apply a bland astringent soothing cream.

D.9.5 bismuth subgallate (Anusol)

Treat: ointment or suppository twice daily (sometimes incorporate hydrocortisone (HC) and local anaesthetic).

D.10 SKIN ANTISEPTICS

Crystals of brilliant green, gentian violet, potassium permanganate and methylene blue make weakly antiseptic solutions; their bright colour aids a placebo effect.

Antiseptic concentrates (diluted with cooled boiled water) cleanse and disinfect closed skin and open wounds but may cause sensitivity; they have little or no advantage over washing with copious water and soap.

D.10.1 povidone-iodine (Betadine).

D.11 SKIN APPLICATIONS

Itching (pruritus) is often less bearable than pain and can drive a person crazy, where possible treat the cause first. Topical antihistamines and local anaesthetics work poorly and may cause skin sensitization, especially antibiotic creams. Oral antihistamines subdue allergic skin rashes. Most wounds and minor burns heal when left open to the air to dry; nothing betters cleaning with soap and water. Many skin infections respond to systemic antibiotics.

Steroid creams suppress skin inflammation (especially eczema), and relieve symptoms but do not cure the condition. Beware of a rebound worsening effect on ceasing treatment. Side-effects may arise with long-continued use.

Clotrimazole is used against fungi, e.g. monilia and tinea.

Sunscreens filter out the ultra-violet spectrum that causes burning red erythema.

D.11.1 betamethasone (Betnovate) 0.1% cream – a strong steroid

Treat: apply thinly 2 to 3 times daily

D.11.2 clotrimazole (Canesten)

Treat: apply 2 to 3 times daily, continuing for 1 to 2 weeks after the lesions have healed

s/e: skin irritation and sensitivity

D.11.3 para-amino benzoic (PABA) esters

Treat: apply 1 hour before exposure to sun and frequently thereafter

D.11.4 calamine ointment

Treat: apply to itching skin

D.11.5 lip salve

Treat: apply on under-side of nose as well as lips

D.11.6 methyl salicylate muscle rub

massage produces soothing 'deep heat'.

D.12 EYES

Chloramphenicol is a broad spectrum antibiotic both for eye and ear

Dexamethasone is a strong steroid against iritis

Homatropine, a mydriatic, dilates the pupil for about 24 hours and eases reflex iris spasm pain in corneal lesions

Amethocaine local anaesthetic acts within seconds and lasts a couple of hours; it delays healing so avoid long term use.

D.12.1 chloramphenicol

Treat: apply 1% ointment every 6 hours

D.12.2 dexamethasone

Treat: apply 0.1% ointment every 6 hours

D.12.3 homatropine

Treat: apply 2% drops twice daily

D.12.4 amethocaine

Treat: apply 1% drops as indicated.

D.13 EARS

Chloramphenicol ointment put in the ear melts and flows through the canal; can be used for both ear and eye.

D.13.1 chloramphenicol

Treat: apply 1% ointment every 6 hours.

D.14 NOSE

Phenylephrine decongestant takes effect immediately and lasts 4 to 6 hours.

D.14.1 phenylephrine

Treat: 2.5% nose drops as needed.

D.15 THROAT

At high altitude the cold dry atmosphere parches the throat so lozenges are needed in bulk.

D.16 TEETH

A lost filling can be a serious problem; insert oil of cloves into the cavity, then a temporary filling to stave off the pain.
D.16.1 oil of cloves
D.16.2 temporary filling.

D.17 LOCAL ANAESTHETIC

D.17.1 xylocaine 2% for injection.

D.18 ORAL REHYDRATION SOLUTIONS

Fluid by mouth helps redress upset body water balance resulting from diarrhoea, shock, burns and dehydration. Give sips of fluid, enough to quench thirst but not to cause vomiting.

Sachets for making suitable solution are available and convenient, but the WHO formula is simple to make and contains most of the essential sugar and salts dissolved in 1 litre of boiled or disinfected water:

glucose	20g = 1½ tsp honey or corn syrup
sodium chloride	3.5g = ½ tsp table salt
sodium bicarbonate	2.5g = ½ tsp baking soda
potassium chloride	1.5g = ¼ tsp or 2 cups of orange, apple, or other fruit juice.

D.19 WATER PURIFICATION

D.19.1 iodine – 1 tab in 2 litres, or iodine tincture (2%) – 4 to 10 drops per litre
D.19.2 chlorine – Halozone – 2 tabs in 1 litre, or household bleach – 2 drops in 1 litre.

Routes for giving medications

MOUTH (ORAL)

Oral medicines – as pills, tablets or capsules – are convenient. Liquids, though better absorbed, are unsuitable for wilderness medical kits because of weight and the danger of breakage and freezing. Oral medication is useless if the person is unconscious, vomiting, or suffering from severe indigestion and nausea; it is absorbed most quickly on an empty stomach, but sometimes because of acid constituents, must accompany food. The lining of the mouth, especially under the tongue, absorbs some pills well, e.g. morphine sulphate and glyceryl trinitrate, but the taste is bitter. The stomach absorbs unevenly, taking a minimum of 2 hours; reaching an adequate therapeutic blood level may take 24–48 hours (especially in the case of antibiotics). Hence the onset of action is slow by mouth compared with the i/v route (fastest), i/m (faster), or s/c (fast).

INJECTION

Before giving any injection read carefully, and ideally have a companion check, the label on the ampoule or vial, to make sure that the intended drug is correct in name, strength, and dilution. Wash hands. Cover the neck of the ampoule with a piece of cloth or tissue so any glass broken accidentally cannot cut your fingers. Clean the top of a rubber-capped vial with an alcohol swab. Assemble syringe and needle directly from their sterile packages without contaminating either. Draw a measured dose of fluid into the syringe, hold it vertically needle upwards, and expel any air bubbles. To get the feel of thrusting a needle through skin (horror!) practise on an orange, which has a similar consistency.

Intramuscular injection (i/m):
sites of choice are:

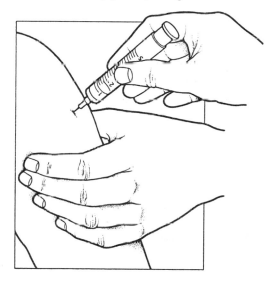

Injection sites

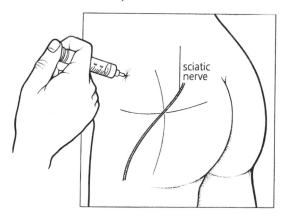

sciatic nerve

– over the upper outer arm a hand's-breadth below the tip
of the shoulder (deltoid muscle)
– upper outer quarter of the buttock (to avoid the sciatic
nerve)
– front of the thigh midway between hip bone (iliac crest)
and kneecap.

After cleaning, pinch the skin widely between thumb and
fingers of one hand; hold the loaded syringe like a dart in
the other hand and thrust it up to the hilt of the needle deep
into the muscle. Pull back on the plunger to ensure the
needle is not in a blood vessel. If blood returns into the
barrel of the syringe withdraw the needle and start again; if
clear, push steadily and slowly on the plunger until emptied.
Withdraw the needle and clean the skin with the same swab,
rubbing vigorously to spread the injected drug and to ease
the discomfort of suddenly distending the tissues.

Subcutaneous injection (s/c):
choose lax skin such as the abdomen or above the collar
bone. Adrenaline is given s/c; morphine can be.

Prepare as for i/m injection above. Pinch the skin only,
and insert the needle at an angle until you feel a 'give' as it
enters the fat layer just below skin but above muscle. Pull
back on the plunger, look for blood – and if none appears,
inject slowly.

Intravenous injection (i/v):
this route gets an injected drug into action fastest, but the
effect is sudden and potent, so should only be used by someone familiar with the action and possible complications of
giving the drug i/v. The technique can be learned with practice. This summary of the technique is a reminder for doctors
who have spent time away from the sharp end of practice.

To make the veins stand out tie a tourniquet round the upper
arm. Ask the person to clench and open a fist repeatedly, hang

an arm over the side of the bed, immerse a hand in warm water, or cover it with a hot, wet towel. Seek the largest vein on the back of the forearm for first choice, on the back of the hand next, in the crook of the elbow if you can't find one elsewhere. Clean the skin. Stretch it over the vein tightly with one hand and pierce it to the side of the engorged vein, angle the needle and advance it through the vein wall being careful not to pierce the opposite wall. Blood will return into the syringe if the needle is in place. Undo the tourniquet! Inject the required amount of drug slowly. Withdraw the needle, swab the site and keep firm pressure for a minute. If the i/v site swells the needle has probably punctured the vein and the drug has run into the tissues – it then becomes a s/c injection instead, so leave it and await results patiently.

3

AIRWAY BLOCK

When the tongue falls against the back of the throat (pharynx), the voice box (larynx) goes into spasm, or if a pool of saliva, blood, or vomit forms, the airway becomes blocked and must be opened immediately. A victim of severe trauma or heart attack who is not breathing is likely already to be dead, so only start to resuscitate if recovery and rescue are possible.

Look, listen, feel

If you cannot detect breathing: *look* carefully at the person's chest and upper abdomen; *listen* with your ear; and *feel* with your cheek against his nose and mouth. A partially blocked airway sounds like croaking or snoring. Froth may appear at the mouth, and the lips are tinged blue (cyanosis) instead of their normal pink colour. Obstructed breathing causes shallow chest movement and the spaces between the ribs suck inwards with each breath. Place your ear against his chest to listen better.

In quiet, normal breathing air passes through the nose; the mouth remains closed, almost completely filled by the tongue lying against the teeth and hard palate. The base of the tongue is fixed to the lower jaw (mandible) and when fully protruded shows only about ⅓ of its total bulk. The relaxed tongue of a

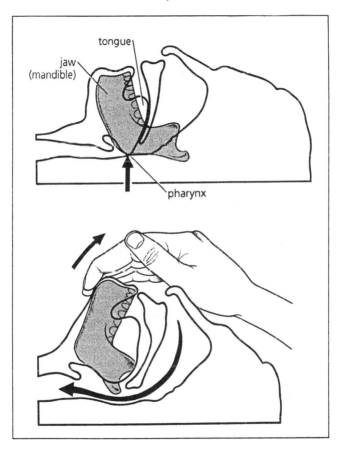

Airway and tongue anatomy

supine unconscious person falls back against the pharynx, obstructs the airway and may even form an air-tight block, like a cork.

An unconscious person can still vomit, but may have no laryngeal, cough, or swallowing reflexes to prevent food, water, blood, saliva and vomit from going down the wrong way. Inhaled, these substances irritate the lungs to secrete fluid, which obstructs gas exchange between blood and air.

Act: unblock an obstructed airway with utmost speed. Tilt the head, lift the jaw, and turn the victim into the draining position; then remove secretions, insert a plastic airway, and fix the tongue. Hope he will not need an endotracheal tube, cricothyrotomy or tracheotomy – read on.

Head tilt:
tilt the head back slightly to straighten out the trachea, which may be kinked if the neck is flexed with the chin on the chest. One hand presses gently on the forehead, the other lifts the chin. Even if the neck is injured, more important is to prevent the victim dying from suffocation than to worry about worsening a damaged neck, serious though that may be.

Jaw lift:
lift the lower jaw with three fingers under the chin so the tongue moves forwards with it. With three fingers of each hand widely spaced, grasp the jaw and push it skywards (not merely closing the upper and lower teeth). It is easier to lift the jaw with the person lying supine, resting your elbows on the ground; but also learn how to do it in the draining position. Holding the jaw with only one hand frees the other, but requires skill.

Draining position:
turn the person on one side – head lower than body. Tilt the

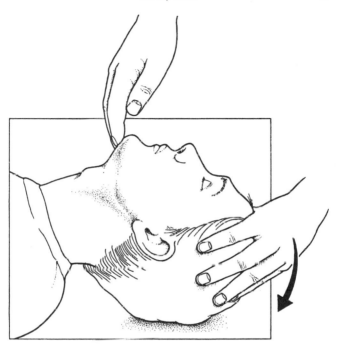

Head tilt

head to straighten the neck and avoid kinking the windpipe (trachea). The tongue will fall forward by gravity so any fluid can drain. This position has many names: coma, recovery, tonsil, but a single aim – drainage. Once fluid is inhaled into the lung, drainage is ineffectual and the victim may drown in his own juices.

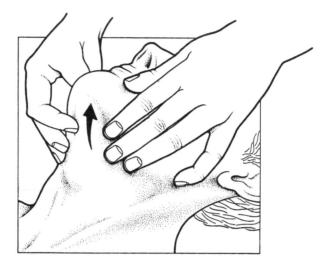

Jaw lift

Finger sweep:
wrap your finger in a piece of cloth, and scoop out of the person's mouth any vomited food, blood clot, or avalanche powder-snow. Don't remove well-fitting dentures. A conscious person may clench tight his teeth and jaws but can maintain his own airway; so do not risk breaking teeth by prying them open. The crossed finger manoeuvre (see page 53) makes holding the jaw open single-handedly easier, provided there is not much resistance.

Suck out:
to remove fluid or secretions from the airway pass a flexible tube far back in the throat, suck on it and spit out the

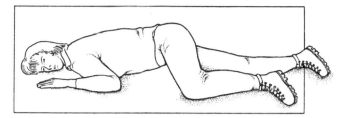

Drainage position

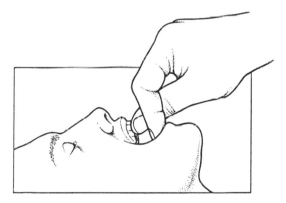

Crossed finger manoeuvre

material. If secretions have pooled near the larynx this unpleasant task may be life-saving. Rescue teams should carry foot-operated suction pumps.

Tongue fix:
if the chin and tongue of an unconscious person persist in

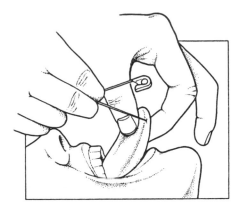

Tongue fix

falling back (e.g. during a stretcher carry) and if you have no mechanical airway, thrust a large safety pin through the tip of the tongue, tie a piece of string to it, pull it firmly forwards and attach it to his belt; this seemingly brutal action guarantees a clear airway leaving minimal damage. Should the victim regain consciousness, quickly remove the pin so he can thank you properly.

MECHANICAL AIRWAYS
Insert an airway if breathing remains obstructed despite all the above. A person who resists, gags on, or fights a mechanical airway, does not need one because he must be conscious enough to safeguard his own airway unaided.

Oral airway:
carry a small, light, cheap plastic oral airway in your first-aid kit. Open the mouth wide, pull the tongue forwards, and insert the airway (moistened to slide more easily) with the

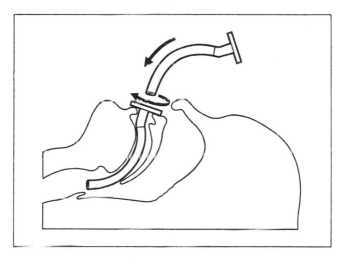

Inserting oral airway

curve pointing towards the roof of the mouth; then rotate
it. The end curves over the back of the tongue keeping open
the pharynx. The metal tooth guard prevents a half-
conscious person biting it closed; the flange stops it slipping
down the throat.

2-ended oral airway: makes mouth-to-mouth resuscitation less distasteful. An airway with a one-way valve and a cheek guard can
be attached to a self-inflating bag.
naso-pharyngeal airway: pass a well-greased tube about 15cm long
gently through one nostril, thread it backwards until the rubber
flange lies against the nose (to prevent it being sucked into the
lung). The end should lie in the pharynx and provide a clear
airway past the obstructing tongue.
endotracheal tube: passing an endotracheal tube into the larynx by

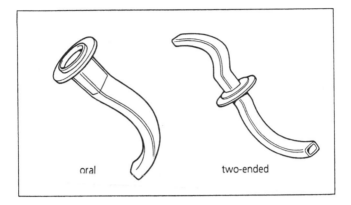

oral   two-ended

Mechanical airways

a skilled person can be life-saving; forcing one clumsily causes spasm of the vocal cords, which may only relax when the victim is about to die. Endotracheal intubation once learned is never forgotten; serious rescuers should ask a local hospital anaesthetist to teach them how.

Using a laryngoscope to light the way, pass the tube through the vocal cords to lie in the trachea. An inflated cuff seals off the trachea and prevents anything being inhaled into the lungs. Thereby during evacuation the airway remains open in all positions of the head and neck. There is no hurry to remove a modern, soft cuffed-tube. The lungs are aerated most efficiently when the tube is attached to a self-inflating resuscitation bag, preferably connected to a supply of oxygen.

CRICOTHYROTOMY

Cricothyrotomy might save a person about to die from airway block unrelieved by a mechanical airway or an endotracheal tube. Such bold surgery requires skill, good judgement, and courage, but is acceptable in dire emergencies in competent hands.

Push a wide-bore #14 gauge needle directly into the trachea through the cricothyroid membrane, easily found in the mid-line of the neck 1cm (½") below the prominence of the larynx and above the cricoid cartilage. The thyroid gland and other vital neck structures are well lateral to the cricothyroid membrane, and the posterior ring of the cricoid cartilage should protect the oesophagus behind. Air will hiss out if the needle enters the trachea. A few puffs of air (or better, oxygen) should aerate the lungs enough to relax any vocal cord spasm.

If using a knife, cut transversely through the skin and the cricothyroid membrane, spread the wound, and slide a soft-cuffed tube through the hole into the trachea. Pre-packed, sterile, disposable cricothyrotomy tubes are available commercially.

Tracheotomy should only be done in a surgical operating room.

Absent breathing

RESCUE BREATHING
If the person is unable to breathe despite an open airway, blow oxygen into the lungs urgently – but only if there is a reasonable chance of recovery and rescue. If he does not start breathing on his own after ½ hour, stop resuscitation (unless expert help is expected imminently) because your efforts are fruitless and exhausting, and will imperil your own retreat.

Mouth-to-mouth:
check that the heart is beating before proceeding. It is easier to do mouth-to-mouth with the person turned on his back than lying on one side. Tilt the head and wipe away debris and secretions in his mouth. Place your mouth tightly over

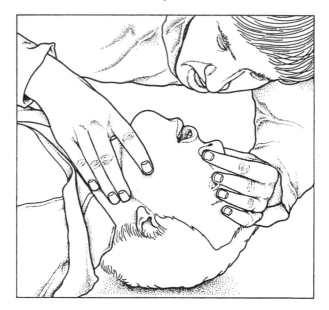

Mouth-to-mouth

the victim's mouth (preferably using a mouth guard protection), and exhale fully every 5 seconds while pinching his nostrils to stop air escaping. Watch his chest, which will rise if the lungs are inflating adequately; about ¼ to ½ litre of air should move with each breath. His own lung elasticity will expel the air. If his mouth is injured breathe into his nose instead, holding his lips closed the while. Your own nasty expired breath, although not as good as pure air, may change the victim's colour from blue to pink. After 4 minutes without oxygen the brain suffers irreparable damage although the victim may partly recover consciousness later.

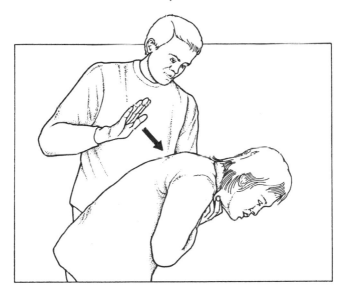

Back blows

Self-expanding hand-inflated bellows:
air is sucked through a one-way valve and expelled at the other
end. The bellows can attach to a face mask over the nose and
mouth, or connect to a mechanical airway. Inflation is easier work
than mouth-to-mouth breathing and can be continued for longer.

CHOKING
A person choking from airway block caused by a foreign
body grasps his throat with both hands, goes blue in the
face and cannot breathe, speak or cough.

Act: open the victim's mouth, grasp his jaw and pull it

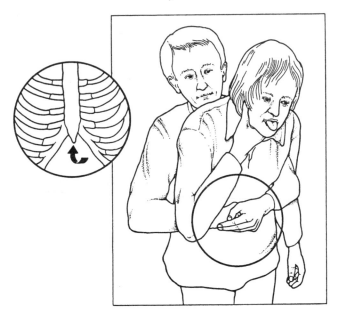

Heimlich manoeuvre

forward. Sweep the index finger of your other hand as far
back in the throat as possible, and hook out any foreign
material. Strike 5 sharp blows rapidly with the heel of the
hand in between his shoulder blades while supporting his
breastbone (sternum) with your other hand.

Abdominal thrusts (Heimlich manoeuvre):
stand behind the victim, wrap your arms around his waist
(making sure not to press on his ribs) and grasp with one
hand the closed fist of your other hand placed over the
upper abdomen. Give 5 upward thrusts (relaxing completely

between each) strong enough to force air out of the lungs and to dislodge the obstruction, but not so violent as to rupture an internal organ. Repeat 5 cycles; if still no response, repeat with the victim lying supine on the ground before giving up.

4

HEART STOP

The commonest cause of heart stop, even in the mountains, is heart attack (myocardial infarction); the heart can also stop after severe trauma, near-drowning, deep hypothermia or a lightning strike. In remote places heart stop caused by trauma is usually fatal.

A summary of cardio-pulmonary resuscitation (CPR) is given here because it is one of the skills expected of all first-aiders; but in wilderness far from help its chance of success is nearly zero. So I am tempted to banish this section to the end of the book and print it small, but fear of outcry from enthusiastic 'hands-on' rescuers has persuaded me reluctantly to leave it in place. Should you want to brush up on your CPR (especially swimming pool lifeguards), take a practical course – better than just reading about it.

Feel, listen, look

Absent pulse or heart sounds:
   carotid pulse – *feel* in the neck by sliding your finger tips into the groove between the victim's windpipe (trachea) and neck muscles at the level of the Adam's Apple (larynx). *Listen* with your ear pressed against the front of his bare chest to the left side of the breastbone (sternum); the heart sounds like a distant 'lub-dup, lub-dup, lub-dup'.
   radial pulse – *feel* at the wrist, but it is unreliable because the rescuer's cold fingers searching for it under tight anorak

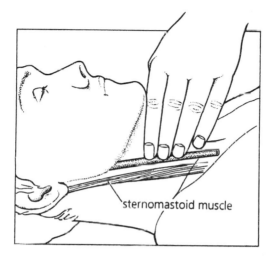

Carotid artery pulse

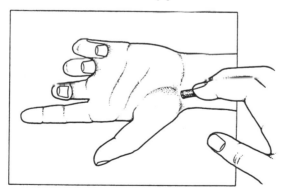

Radial artery pulse

cuffs may give the false impression that the heart has stopped.

femoral pulse – alternatively feel in the groin halfway between the pubic bone, and the wing of the pelvis (iliac crest).

Absent breathing:
listen with your ear near his mouth; feel the chest for movement of air.

Hypothermia:
feel for 30 seconds or more because the pulse may be glacially slow in hypothermia.

Unconsciousness:
the person looks deathly pale, does not respond to command or pain, and pupils slowly dilate and fail to constrict to the stimulus of light.

Act: Start CPR immediately because irreversible brain damage occurs after the heart and breathing have stopped for 4 minutes. A person who is ice-cold and appears dead may be hypothermic, so try to rewarm and resuscitate him because his brain function may be protected by the cold.

Rescue breathing:
if there is a pulse but no breathing – start mouth-to-mouth rescue breathing immediately with 2 quick, full breaths, allowing the lungs to deflate fully between breaths. Then check the pulse; if it is beating, continue rescue breathing about once every 5 seconds.

Chest compression:
if there is a pulse – lay the victim horizontal, or slightly head down on a hard, flat surface and raise his feet on a rucksack to get the best gravity feed for venous blood to return to the brain and central circulation. Kneel beside him and feel

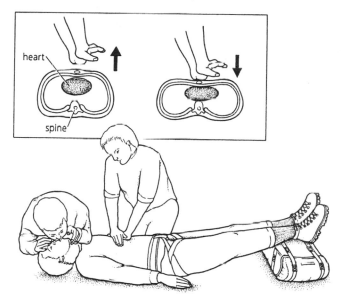

Chest compression

for the notch where ribs and sternum join. Place the heel of your hand two finger-breadths above the notch, with your other hand on top so the fingers of both hands are parallel and interlocked. Do not rest on the chest. With your arms straight and shoulders vertically over your hands, press down smoothly, regularly and evenly with sufficient force to depress the sternum 4 to 5cm and squeeze the heart enough to pump blood to the brain. Fractured ribs can be dealt with later. Release the pressure completely after each compression to allow the heart to refill, but do not lose contact with the sternum.

Single rescuer:
15 to 2 sequence. Compress the chest 15 times, pressing more than once every second. Then give 2 quick, full rescue breaths lasting 4–5 seconds. Feel the carotid pulse after 1 minute, then every 3 minutes, to see if the heart has restarted; if it has, stop compressing immediately, but continue rescue breathing until he breathes normally.

2 rescuers:
5 to 1 sequence. Compress the chest once every second while an assistant gives a swift rescue breath at the upstroke of every 5th compression without interrupting compressions. Check the pulse as above. Teamwork and good timing need practice.

Once started, continue CPR until, hopefully, spontaneous heartbeat and breathing return. The person becomes warmer, blue lips and pale skin turn pink, and large dilated pupils return to normal. Watch him closely for a relapse. CPR is hard work and ½ hour is about as long as most people can manage on their own before handing over to someone else. If the heart does not restart within this time it probably never will.

5

HEAD INJURY

Generally speaking, not-so-bad head injuries tend to get better, those with bad head injuries tend to get worse and die. Less than 1% of head injuries need surgery; those that do, need it at once. Do not be tempted to meddle. A Swiss army knife, an ice screw, or the pick of an ice axe, wielded in the field by a neurosurgeon could be life-saving; in unskilled hands they would probably be lethal weapons.

Prevent the victim dying of, or being harmed by, other causes, the most important of which are further rock fall and ice avalanche, airway block, neck injury, and bleeding. Climbers' hard hats, like motor cycle crash-helmets and car seat-belts, reduce the numbers of serious head injuries; sensible people use them.

Airway block (see chapter 3)

Snoring, rattling breathing is a sign of a blocked airway, not of head injury. Tilt the head, lift the jaw, and turn the victim into the draining position with the head slightly downhill. Don't leave him lying on his back for fear of worsening a neck injury, because his tongue will sink backwards, block the airway and kill him. Also he may inhale vomit or blood trickling down the back of the throat from an associated face or nose injury. Insert an oral airway. If he is deeply unresponsive, or if his face is badly smashed, with lacerations around the mouth, a fractured jaw and dislodged teeth, simply holding the jaw will probably not keep his airway open.

If the mouth is unharmed pass an endotracheal tube using a laryngoscope. If the mouth is injured insert a naso-pharyngeal airway (possible without direct vision if done with skill). If neither method is successful consider cricothyrotomy to prevent suffocation.

Neck injury

A victim of head injury may also have injured his neck, so examine it carefully and determine if feeling in his arms and legs is normal, and if his bladder is working. Place a cervical collar, and strap him to an improvised spinal board to avoid unnecessary movement.

Bleeding

The scalp and face can bleed profusely and alarmingly but this indicates poorly the gravity of the head injury.

SCALP WOUNDS

Act: stop bleeding by firm pressure over the wound with a dressing pad – any clean cotton material placed on top of a sterile gauze square. Do not remove the first blood-soaked dressing because you will disturb fresh clot; just add more dressings on top as needed. When bleeding is controlled, wash and clean the wound with plenty of water, removing blot clots, dirt and hair. If necessary, cut away some hair to get a better view and access to the scalp. Scalp wounds usually heal well without suturing; instead you can hold the edges together by tying small bundles of twisted hair across the wound. An open skull wound, or a suspected depressed fracture, needs a doughnut dressing – a ring pad that presses around the wound edge on undamaged skull without pressure on the centre.

Face wounds:
usually heal well; but to get the best scar appose the edges accurately with Steristrips or tape. A plastic surgeon can tidy up an ugly scar later.

FACIAL FRACTURE

Facial bones may be broken in several places in a bad smash. Suspect a fracture if the person has double vision and a sunken (black) eye, a flattened bruised cheek, a step in the smooth lower rim of the orbit, or if chewing is painful and the bite is abnormally uneven.

Act: patch the bad eye to correct double vision; feed a fluid diet through a straw until the jaw can be fixed by a surgeon.

JAW DISLOCATION

Act: relax the jaws with lorazepam (D.5.1). Support the lower jaw with the fingers of both hands, place your thumbs over his molars (padded to prevent him biting them), then push steadily down and backwards. The jaw should slide back into place (see diagram page 70).

TEMPORAL ARTERY LACERATION

A minor cut over the temple can sever the artery which runs close under the skin over the skull (felt 2cm above and in front of the ear hole). If the cut end spurts, seize it with forceps and tie it with cotton; otherwise pressure will have to suffice until the artery retracts and goes into spasm.

A conscious victim of head injury can respond to questions that will help make a diagnosis; if unconscious, he will need total care.

*   *   *

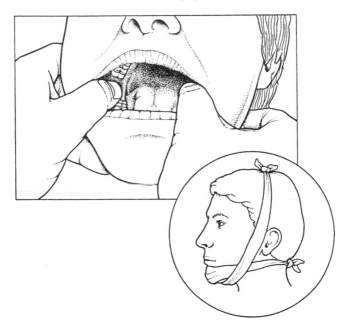

Reducing dislocated jaw

Care of an unconscious victim

After dealing with immediate life-threatening conditions of airway block, neck injury and bleeding, attend to the following:

Restless behaviour:
may result from brain disturbance, pain, or a full bladder; he may need restraint.

Pain:
Treat: codeine (D.1.3); do not use morphine, which depresses breathing, alters consciousness, and constricts the pupils thereby disguising a vital observation (see page 33).

Bladder:
a bursting bladder causes a person to thrash about, so encourage peeing by stroking the inside of the thigh and pouring water loudly from one cup to another. If this fails consider a suprapubic stab with a wide-bore needle (see page 168).

Eyes:
lubricate with any eye ointment to prevent the cornea developing ulcers from dry air exposure.

Skin:
prevent bedsores by turning the victim every 2 hours and keeping bowel and groin areas scrupulously clean. Infection of raw skin can cause blood poisoning (septicaemia), a common cause of death in head injuries.

Feeding:
an unconscious person cannot feed himself; if neglected over several days he may become starved and dehydrated.

Pass a naso-gastric tube with a funnel attached by which sustenance can flow directly into the stomach. Plain water is better than nothing. Desist if you suspect a basal skull fracture because the tube may penetrate into the brain.

MECHANISM OF HEAD INJURY

The brain is composed of soft nerve tissue suspended in cerebro-spinal fluid (CSF), which cushions movement within the rigid skull. Blood vessels around the brain may tear in severe head injury causing pressure to rise inside the skull.

Primary brain injury:
caused at the moment of impact by displacement, distortion, and stretching of brain within the skull.

Skull fracture:
may be closed or open (compound) when clear CSF may leak from the nose or ears, or directly from the wound. Infection may be lethal, so treat any open fracture with a sulpha antibiotic which can cross the blood-brain barrier; otherwise Rx: co-trimoxazole (D.2.2).

TYPES OF BRAIN DAMAGE

Concussion:
a trivial blow on the head deranges the brain so the victim falls unconscious briefly. After rest, recovery may be quick and complete. The speed at which someone recovers after seeing stars, or being knocked out, indicates the severity of the injury and the final outcome. He may appear normal; but anyone unconscious from a head injury, however briefly, must not walk unattended, even if he considers his injury trivial.

Clot compression:
after a trifling knock on the head the person may improve and appear quite normal for a short while (lucid interval) and wish to continue the expedition. But continued bleeding, or swelling of the brain itself, causes pressure within the skull to rise. The person complains of severe headache, then becomes drowsy, slips into coma, and will die unless a surgeon quickly drills a trephine hole in the skull to release blood under pressure.

Treat: dexamethasone (D.4.2) may temporarily reduce the pressure, but rescuers must evacuate the victim fast to a surgeon.

Contusion, laceration, and local damage:
severe trauma may bruise or mangle local areas of the brain
causing irritation with fits of twitching of the opposite limbs;
these may spread into general grand mal epileptic seizures
when the victim may die from airway block. Occasionally
the limbs are paralysed on the opposite side of the body.

Severe, diffuse injury:
the person is deeply unconscious from the time of injury and
unable to keep an open airway without help. He may roll
about in a purposeless manner and fall again unless prevented.

Observe and record

After taking urgent steps to prevent the victim of head injury
dying, start accurate hourly recording of changing trends in
his level of consciousness and his clinical progress. Your
notes may help the surgeon, who will see him for the first
time some hours later, decide whether to operate immediately to relieve pressure from bleeding within the skull. If
you don't write things down during the tumult of the rescue,
afterwards you won't remember accurately:

Ask the victim, if conscious or, if not, ask a witness about:
– details of the accident: exact time, length of fall or falling
  objects, roped or helmeted
– duration of unconsciousness, if any
– alteration in behaviour or level of consciousness
– convulsions
– hypothermia (possible at the accident site)
– any known medical problems

Look for a Medic-Alert bracelet or medallion detailing known
illnesses and current medication. Convulsions or uncon-

sciousness, before or after the injury, may result from illness unrelated to the head injury (e.g. epilepsy, diabetes, heart attack). Smell the breath for alcohol, or the sweet acetone odour of diabetes.

The head:
remove any hat or helmet and *look* at the whole head; *feel* for blood pooled under the neck. Wash wounds with soap and water and remove blood clot, hair, and pieces of foreign material. *Look* for a fracture in the depths of the wound, but never probe it and risk introducing infection, or worse, penetrating the brain through an open skull fracture. A large boggy swelling under the scalp, in the absence of an open wound, suggests blood collecting at the site of a skull fracture. The tongue may be bitten during a convulsion.

Clear fluid oozing or dripping from the nose or ears may be cerebro-spinal fluid leaking from a fracture at the base of the skull. Bleeding from the nose or ears, when not caused by obvious external injury, may also come from inside the skull. Both are signs of grave injury and need urgent surgical attention.

Treat: antibiotics (D.2) in maximum doses.

Level of response: this is based on the Glasgow Coma Scale which is used internationally to estimate the level of response and replaces vague, confusing terms of yore like 'stupor' and 'black-out'. Noting the scale over several hours will show if the response level is becoming lighter and approaching normal, or is deepening because of increasing pressure on the brain from bleeding or swelling.

GLASGOW COMA SCALE (modified)

Eyes (E) open:

spontaneously	4
on command	3
in response to pain	2
remain closed	1

Movement (M):

        on command   6

        in response to pain   4

        no response   1

Speech (S):

        answers and converses normally   5

        is confused   4

        uses inappropriate words   3

        makes incomprehensible sounds   2

        no response   1

Scoring

8 to 7 total = will probably survive

     6 total = outcome doubtful

5 to 4 total = will probably die

A simple record might look something like this:-

Date	Time	E	M	S	Total	Pulse	Notes
11.4.98	1430	4	4	3	11	80	Restless
11.4.98	1500	3	4	3	10	88	R. Pupil enlarging

Eyes:

when the brain of an unconscious person is compressed by an enlarging pool of blood, the pupil dilates on the side of the clot. This tells the surgeon on which side to drill a trephine hole. If pressure is not relieved the opposite pupil becomes paralysed. Two fixed dilated pupils indicate the victim is almost surely dead.

    If one pupil of an awake, alert person is bigger than the other it may be because light is coming more strongly from one side, the pupil may have been like that since birth, or because of a blow on the eye (traumatic mydriasis). If a person blinks when you wave a hand close in front of his eye, the visual pathways to the brain must be intact. Touching the cornea with a wisp of cotton wool should cause reflex blinking.

Ophthalmoscope examination
   Papilloedema occurs in advanced cranial pressure
   Retinal haemorrhages suggest bleeding owing to sudden increase in intracranial pressure from a primary brain injury.

Pulse, breathing, and temperature:
raised pressure inside the skull slows the pulse and raises the blood pressure (opposite to shock in which the pulse quickens and blood pressure falls). Breathing becomes irregular and periodic (Cheyne-Stokes). In severe head injury the heat-regulating centre fails and the temperature may soar to 41°C (106°F), or more. Cool the person vigorously with cold water, ice or snow.

Sensation and power:
loss of feeling to light touch, or numbness and tingling, may indicate damage to the peripheral nerves, spine or brain. Progressive one-sided weakness suggests localized brain damage, and the limbs may become partially or completely paralysed.

Coma

Consider other causes of coma in an unconscious person who tells no story, nor shows any sign of head injury. *Look* for a Medic-Alert bracelet or medallion. But remember that the victim may also have struck his head while falling unconscious for other reasons.

FAINTING

A simple faint is a brief drop in blood pressure with transient loss of consciousness. The cause may be pain, excitement, fear, sight of blood, or prolonged standing (in heat). The person feels dizzy, goes cold and clammy, and passes out crumpling to the ground.

Act: lay him flat, head down/feet up (or, if sitting, head between the knees). Loosen tight clothing, and put a cold cloth on the forehead. Examine carefully for other possible causes of coma (see below).

EPILEPSY

In seizure an epileptic suddenly lets out a cry and falls rigid to the ground. He may hold his breath temporarily and go blue, twitch, jerk violently, roll his eyes, froth at the mouth, bite his tongue and pee his pants. The seizure usually passes off in a few minutes; he wakes up but shortly after falls into a deep sleep of recovery, which can be mistaken for coma. He may have a headache on waking.

Act: prevent him injuring himself. Do not wedge anything between his teeth to stop tongue-biting; if the teeth are clenched he will be conscious enough to safeguard his own airway. Turn him into the recovery position

Treat: lorazepam (D.5.1) 1–2mg i/v would work as an anti-convulsant [diazepam is better], by mouth it acts slowly. For a known epileptic on treatment (usually with phenytoin), double the dose for a day and ensure he takes his pills. Consult a doctor forthwith.

DIABETES

Diabetics do not produce enough insulin, the hormone that allows the body to burn glucose (carbohydrate) as fuel for energy. A severe diabetic requires a calculated amount of

carbohydrate each day and self-administered injections of
insulin, which he must always carry because of possible
delay in returning to camp by weather or travel problems.
Diabetics expecting to burn more fuel than usual, as in a
hard day's exercise, must temporarily increase carbohydrate
intake. Failing to do so may lead to either hypoglycemia
(too little sugar for insulin to work on), or diabetic pre-coma
(too much sugar) when insulin or oral diabetic medication
must be increased. Either of these two conditions may cause
a slide into coma. Distinguishing which is which is vital
because their treatment is contrary.

	Hypoglycemia	*Diabetic pre-coma*
onset	sudden in healthy person	gradual in ill diabetic
appearance	sweaty & faint	warm, flushed, thirsty
tongue and skin	moist, cool & clammy	dry
breath smell	normal	ketones (nail varnish)
urine taste	bitter	sweet & copious
Treat:	glucose	insulin

STROKE

Although usually restricted to older people, the young may
suffer strokes, especially as a complication of high blood
pressure, diabetes or altitude. The person complains of
severe headache, then loses consciousness and may convulse. The head and eyes turn to one side, the opposite
side of the body becomes paralysed, partially or completely.
Breathing is heavy with snoring and may be periodic
(Cheyne-Stokes).

Act: evacuate urgently (as for all the above serious conditions).

DRUG OVERDOSE

The breath gives the story away when the cause is alcohol (except for odourless vodka). Consider also narcotics, barbiturates, benzodiazepines, social drugs, wild plants and mushrooms.

Act. stomach wash-out (page 181).

ETC.

also think of:

- shock from heart failure, severe injury, bleeding, spinal injury
- hypothermia (page 220), heat stroke (page 127), avalanche asphyxia and near-drowning (all obvious from the circumstances).

6

SPINE INJURY

Care of the airway is paramount in all victims of neck injury, so gently tilt the head and lift the jaw. Some first-aiders are brain-washed against moving a neck injury victim under any circumstances with the result that he may die of airway block, which kills more often than the neck injury itself.

Neck fracture and/or dislocation

Suspect a fracture and/or dislocation of the neck if the victim has been, or still is, unconscious; fell from a height and injured his head (20% have associated spinal injury); complains of neck pain and tenderness, or holds his neck in an abnormal position; complains of loss of feeling, or tingling and numbness, in the hands or arms; or is unco-operative and mentally changed following head injury or shock.

Act: evacuate the victim without further damage to a hospital where he can be X-rayed, accurately diagnosed and treated by experts. Meanwhile make sure he does not die from other causes. If the spine is fractured and/or dislocated, the neck muscles go into rigid spasm, splinting the neck so you are unlikely to move it further. However, bruising and swelling may spread upwards, affecting progressively higher levels in the spinal cord.

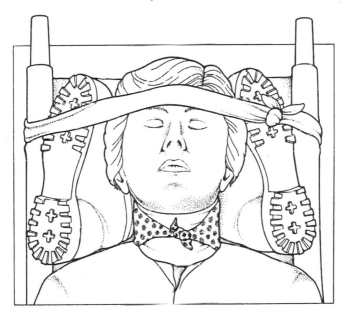

Neck injury

If the victim is awake and alert and wants to move his neck, let him do so; the main reason for splinting the neck is so rescuers cannot unwittingly shift an unstable fracture and/or dislocation. Similarly, if he wants to and can walk, let him.

Splinting:
make a collar of tightly-rolled clothing or newspaper, or a well-padded wire splint about 10cm wide, and secure it around his neck with tape to fit snugly under the chin. Do not try to correct any neck deformity. Place on either side of

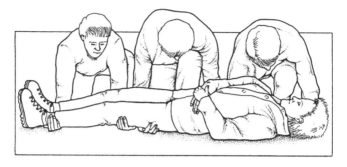

One piece move

the head 2 rolls of clothing or a pair of boots, soles outwards, uppers under the neck. Strap or tape round the forehead to secure the head.

Moving:
give a strong pain-killer before moving the victim. Move him 'in one piece' to avoid displacing any dislocated vertebrae. One rescuer holds the head, one the legs, and another the body; all move together on command so the victim's head does not twist on his shoulders, nor his body on his pelvis. A collar alone will not entirely stabilize the neck, as a spinal board will.

Spinal board:
lay the person flat on a spinal board (improvised from two pack-frames lashed together), or on a stretcher. Tie him firmly to the board so he cannot move, yet the board can still be tipped if he vomits.

AIRWAY – pass a naso-tracheal tube if the victim is not breathing. A naso-gastric tube empties the stomach and reduces the chance of vomiting and aspiration, and prevents distension from gut ileus which often accompanies spinal injury.

Treat: codeine (D.1.3). Avoid narcotic drugs (e.g. morphine) which depress breathing and could kill someone with paralysed chest muscles.

Dexamethasone (D.4.2) may reduce spinal cord swelling.

Back injury

A severe back injury, though unlikely to kill someone outright, may paralyse him from the waist down; thus he may be surprisingly tranquil, feeling as though cut in half. Pain at the site of injury radiates round to the front at that level and shoots down the legs. If he can move fingers and toes, and feel light touch, no nerves are damaged.

Act: – if *conscious* and in full control of his airway, and if he wants to walk by himself, let him do so. If he cannot walk lay him supine on a stretcher.

– if *unconscious*, tie him firmly to a spinal board or stretcher which you can tip should he vomit. Loosen tight clothing; pad bony prominences between his knees and ankles, and body hollows especially behind the neck. He may be more easily moved 'in one piece' with his legs bandaged together.

– if *paralysed*, turn him every hour. He will not feel pain, touch, pressure or temperature. He will lie quite still, so pressure on his skin, normally relieved by shifting body position, will hamper blood flow locally causing painless sores. These can develop in less than an hour and take weeks to heal, especially if infected. Make sure he is not lying on crumpled bedding and clothing. Remove from his pockets hard objects, which cause uneven pressure. If incontinent of bladder or bowels keep him clean and dry with regular hygiene and, if possible, an indwelling catheter.

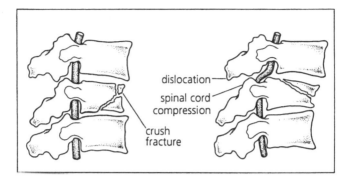

Vertebral fracture

Mechanism of spinal injury

24 vertebrae form a column between skull and pelvis. Forces are transmitted through bony vertebral bodies, behind which lies a protective tunnel for the spinal cord. Nerves leave the spinal cord in descending order – arms, trunk, then legs. Semi-solid discs between the vertebrae act as washers to cushion stresses. Ligaments and powerful muscles stabilize the entire length of the column.

A fractured or dislocated vertebra may damage nerves by pressure and sheering. If the cord is cut across in the neck all four limbs, chest and abdomen will be paralysed (quadriplegia); if the injury is in the middle of the back only the legs and bladder will be affected (paraplegia). Damage to the brain paralyses the opposite side of the body because nerve pathways cross in the brain stem (hemiplegia).

Other spinal problems

WRY NECK (acute torticollis)

Neck muscles go into tight spasm, pulling the head towards one shoulder; it usually occurs after sleeping in an awkward position.

Act: alternate ice packs with heat and gentle massage.

NECK SPRAIN (whiplash)

Whiplash may occur after a fall without visible damage to either head or neck. Severe neck pain may last several months.

Treat: analgesics (D.1), neck collar.

BACK STRAIN (lumbago)

Paraspinal muscles go into painful spasm to splint vertebral joints under strain.

Treat: analgesics (D.1), rest, local heat, avoid heavy lifting or bending.

SLIPPED DISC (sciatica)

A prolapsed disc may press on spinal nerve roots, causing pain and tingling along their distribution – arms if a neck vertebra, legs if lumbar. Pain follows the course of the sciatic nerve; in the buttock, down the back of the thigh, into the calf and possibly as far as the heel or foot. There may be loss of sensation and weakness. The straight leg can only be raised 30° to 40° from the horizontal.

Treat: analgesics (D.1), rest on a firm surface, evacuate if evidence of nerve pressure.

Dexamethasone (D.4.2) may reduce inflammation enough to allow a person to walk out to safety.

PERIPHERAL NERVE INJURIES

Many will eventually return to normal once the offending stimulus is removed.

Lateral femoral cutaneous nerve:
a tight rucksack waist belt may cause loss of feeling in the upper outer thigh.

Brachial plexus palsy:
roping down over the shoulder, and tight rucksack shoulder straps, can press on the brachial plexus. The whole arm may feel numb and weak. If the upper spinal cord only is affected, sensation disappears over the tip of the shoulder, the upper outer arm and the forearm. The elbow cannot move outwards nor can the hand rotate.

Anterior tibial compartment:
'shin splints': overuse causes pain in the muscle over the shin bone (tibia). The foot cannot flex upwards so drops and drags on walking. Sensation is dull on adjacent sides of the big toe and second toe. This is a surgical emergency because the foot drop can be permanent.

Cold injury:
due to hypothermia and frostbite (see page 233).

7

CHEST INJURY

In a serious accident both head and chest can suffer, but the chest injury may pass unnoticed because of a more obvious head injury. Examine both carefully because injuries to either may be fatal – the chest often killing more rapidly.

The chest may be: *crushed (closed injury)* by a tumble onto rock or a tree, a falling stone, or by sudden tightening of a climbing rope or harness after a fall; *punctured (open injury)* by a spike of rock or the pick of an ice axe.

Act: before attempting a diagnosis, keep an open airway. Then seal an open wound with a thick, impermeable dressing like paraffin gauze, plastic kitchen wrap or a plastic bag taped to the skin; splint the chest by binding the victim's arms, bent at the elbow, across his chest. Turn him on his injured side so the weight of his own body splints the chest wall. Pad with clothes to add pressure, but do not bind the chest with strapping or bandages, which diminish breathing movement and encourage pneumonia.

If the airway remains blocked and if cyanosis persists, despite the above, consider endotracheal intubation or cricothyrotomy and artificial ventilation.

Treat: morphine (D.1.4) may be needed to control pain and allow deep breathing. By tradition, narcotics are forbidden in chest injury because they depress respiration; but by relieving pain most people with chest injury breathe better,

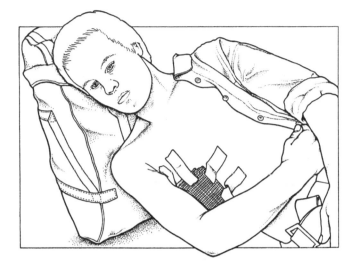

Chest injury nursing position

so be judiciously bold. Morphine can always be reversed with naloxone (D.1.5).

– Antibiotic (D.2.1 or D.2.2) if spit is green or yellow, (always ask the victim to spit into a tissue and look at the colour) or if there is fever – both signs of bronchitis or pneumonia.

– Local anaesthetic (D.17); long-acting [bupivacaine] injected directly into a rib fracture relieves pain for 24 hours, but beware of slipping the needle between the ribs and puncturing the lung

Deep breathing exercises aerate the lungs. To clear secretions, assist coughing by holding the lower chest for support. Inhale steam from a pot of boiling water to liquefy junk in the chest and to help coughing up spit.

Mechanism of chest injury

The chest is a bony cage that acts like a bellows; it expands as the ribs move upwards and outwards, and as the diaphragm moves downwards like a piston. Quiet breathing, done by the diaphragm alone, shows a gentle rise and fall of the upper abdomen. Deep or laboured breathing strains the intercostal muscles (lying between the ribs) and accessory muscles (in the neck). The lungs hang inside the chest cavity, which together with the lung surface is covered by pleura, a membrane that allows the two surfaces to slide over each other without friction. The lung is normally held expanded against the chest wall by a vacuum in the pleural space which, if destroyed, causes the lung to collapse (pneumothorax). The air passages branch like a tree: trachea, bronchi, bronchioles and alveoli, finally the terminal air sacs.

Look, feel, listen

Look at the person in adequate light because inside a coloured tent his unwashed, weather-beaten skin may not show his true hue. Bluish lips (cyanosis) indicate poorly oxygenated blood. Shock pales the face and accentuates cyanosis (present in most climbers above 4,000m/13,000ft). Blood-flecked spittle suggests lung oedema. He may show few signs of injury. Open his clothing to display the whole bare chest. A skin wound or bruising suggests the injured side. The chest moves less on the injured side, and breathing is shallow, irregular and rapid (more than 30 breaths per minute). Severely stressed and painful breathing causes flared nostrils, taut neck muscles, and indrawn intercostal muscles.

Feel the rib cage gently for tenderness and for an unstable segment of chest wall. Place your palms flat on the sides of his bare chest; they should move apart equally with each breath. Crackling of air bubbles in the tissues (surgical emphysema) feels like paper being rustled.

Listen for the croaking sound of obstructed breathing and for a hiss of air escaping from, or the sucking noise of air entering, a chest wound.

Chest wall injury

SIMPLE RIB FRACTURES

Fractured ribs are usually caused by a direct blow, and the resulting bruise can hide a litre of blood. Ribs can fracture spontaneously after a violent bout of coughing (especially at high altitude). Severe pain, especially on breathing, arises from broken rib ends grating against sensitive overlying periosteum. The point of fracture is tender. Fractured ribs heal on their own in 4 to 6 weeks but remain painful during most of that time, especially on deep breathing. Pain leads to shallow breathing and discourages coughing so secretions accumulate and become infected. Yellow or green spit, perhaps with blood, indicates pneumonia, the dreaded complication of chest injury.

Act: rib fractures heal in 4 to 6 weeks and injecting local anaesthetic into the fracture site eases the pain. Do not strap the chest, which restricts breathing and encourages pneumonia.

MULTIPLE RIB FRACTURES

With several fractured ribs the jagged ends may puncture the underlying lung, releasing air into the pleura (pneumothorax), or tear intercostal vessels, pooling blood in the chest (haemothorax). Differentiating between these two in the outdoors is very difficult; as is telling which side of the lung is collapsed (see below).

Fractures of ribs 9, 10 and 11 on the left side may damage

the spleen, on the right side the liver. If the pleural lining of the chest wall is breached, air may leak into the tissues (surgical emphysema) and creep up into the neck where bubbles crackle under the skin.

FLAIL CHEST

Several ribs broken in two places can isolate a segment of chest wall, which moves in an opposing direction during breathing – sucked in on inspiration when the chest normally expands, and bulging on expiration when the chest deflates (paradoxical breathing). The lungs become poorly ventilated and the exchange of gas diminishes causing blue lips (cyanosis) from lack of oxygen. Extra effort to breathe increases the paradoxical movement, making the victim anxious, restless and sweaty.

Act: mild paradoxical breathing may need no treatment. If causing distress, press on the mobile segment of chest wall to splint it. The victim will immediately breathe more easily and become pink again. Tape a wound dressing over the injured ribs and turn him on that side to splint the broken ribs under the weight of his own body and prevent the segment of chest wall moving in and out.

If this fails endotracheal intubation or cricothyrotomy and artificial ventilation may be necessary, along with rapid evacuation to a hospital.

Lung injury

PNEUMOTHORAX OR HAEMOTHORAX

Air or blood can enter the pleural space either from outside by way of a penetrating wound, or from within due to lung ruptured by a fractured rib, or spontaneously in a healthy young person. The vacuum in the pleural space vanishes so the lung, or part of it, collapses. The person becomes breath-less, the pulse rises, and the windpipe deviates from the midline. Imprisoned air may absorb slowly, and the lung re-expand; if not, air may need drawing off through a needle.

To decide which lung is collapsed may be very difficult even with a stethoscope. With the victim breathing through his mouth, breath sounds will be decreased or absent on the affected side. If breathing becomes restricted by a collapsed lung and the victim looks as if he will die, decompress the chest with a needle.

Act: push a wide-bore needle between the ribs at or above the level of the nipple in a line vertically below the mid-point of the axilla between the folds that make the armpit. Point the needle upwards and backwards. (Even if the needle is put into a chest that does not have a pneumothorax the likelihood of injuring the lung is very small indeed.) Allow a hiss of air to escape as he breathes out, then seal the needle with a finger when he breathes in. When all the air appears to have escaped, or blood has been sucked off, pull out the needle and cover the hole with tape. To make a simple one-way valve, tie a condom tightly onto the needle and cut off the rubber tip. Decompression may have to be repeated if the chest fills again.

In hospital, underwater seal drainage with a chest tube is pref-erable for continuous decompression.

TENSION PNEUMOTHORAX (sucking wound)
Urgent, on-the-spot, definitive action is needed because ten-sion pneumothorax kills fast, especially at altitude. A flap of tissue may act as a one-way valve, so more and more air is sucked in and trapped in the pleural space. Pressure in the chest obstructs return of blood to the heart, and also its output. Remove air with a needle (see above).

A simple pneumothorax will not kill, but a tension pneumothorax may.

8

SHOCK

Shock may be caused by severe haemorrhage (internal or external), major burns, profuse vomiting and diarrhoea, overwhelming toxic infection, heart failure, and acute pain or emotion. Shock is a vague term that denotes how the body reacts to life under threat when the circulating blood volume is suddenly reduced and delivers insufficient oxygen for the needs of the vital centres, especially the brain.

In haemorrhagic shock a chain reaction unfolds. Bleeding reduces the volume of blood returning to the heart, which consequently pumps less blood into the circulation. The fall in blood pressure, sensed by receptors in the carotid arteries, speeds the heart and pumps more blood to oxygenate the brain and vital organs. Blood vessels in the extremities of the limbs and the gut clamp down to pool blood in the centre of the body, by-passing the skin which turns cold, clammy, pale and waxy-blue like death.

The victim of shock becomes breathless, thirsty and sick; finally, restless and confused. Prolonged low blood pressure causes irreversible changes in kidneys, adrenals, heart and brain. Unless blood pressure is restored to normal by blood transfusion or intravenous fluids he will fall unconscious and may die. If left too late he may die anyway.

Act: staunch severe bleeding first, then write a record of the victim's state as a baseline to assess whether he is improving or worsening. With hidden bleeding such observations may be the only reliable guide to his condition.

Symptoms and signs of shock

Rapid, feeble pulse:
over 120/minute. Feeling the force of the pulse is only a rough guide to blood pressure, which requires a sphygmo-manometer for accurate measurement.

Pale, cold, clammy, bluish skin:
normal skin is pink and warm.

Capillary blood flow:
a normal big toenail or thumbnail blanches when squeezed, the normal pink colour returning instantly on releasing pressure; the speed of return is a good indicator of blood pressure. Delay of several seconds, along with cold hands, feet, and nose, suggests shock or dehydration.

Restless behaviour:
especially with children in shock.

Thirst:
unquenchable.

Dry, furred tongue:
usually becomes moist again after 2 or 3 days when the person can eat and drink. Encourage drinking fruit juice to restore lost potassium.

Low urine output:
collect and measure all urine passed over a 12 hour period; in dehydration it is dark and concentrated. With adequate

fluid intake a normal person passes more than 25ml of pale, dilute urine each hour.

Sluggish gut movement:
shock can paralyse the intestines, causing vomiting. The gut does not absorb water adequately and the belly may distend (paralytic ileus)

VISIBLE BLOOD LOSS

Estimating blood loss in soaked garments indicates roughly how much blood needs replacing. An egg-cupful of blood on a white shirt looks like an ocean to a lay observer. An injury may appear minor on the front of the victim but a litre or more may have soaked into the clothing and sleeping bag he is lying on.

INVISIBLE BLOOD LOSS

In closed wounds blood spreads along tissue planes causing swelling, or into body cavities displacing and irritating the contents. A fractured femur can bleed a litre into the thigh, and extend up to the hip and down to the knee, making it swell to twice normal girth.

Act: *replace fluid.* If the victim feels thirsty give sips of water enough to quench thirst without making him vomit. After bleeding, osmotic pressure draws body water into the blood to compensate for lost plasma. Fluid by mouth goes some way to help redress upset body water balance, although not as good as replacing blood intravenously.

The WHO formula (D.18) contains all the sugar and salt needed for oral rehydration.

Ideally replace blood with blood, but this is rarely possible outside hospital. If the rescuers bring other i/v fluids (normal saline or Ringer's lactate), start them before evacuating the victim in order to swell his plasma volume and alleviate shock. An i/v drip allows drugs to be administered in finely controlled doses.

Position:
lay the victim head downhill so blood will flow by gravity to
the brain and prevent shock and loss of consciousness. With
head wounds, keep the head up. Using a rucksack, raise the
feet above the level of the heart, thereby returning about 2
litres of blood, pooled in the legs, to the central circulation.
Rest slows the heart; exercise speeds it. Resting the injured
part encourages clotting and prevents a delicate web of early
clot being broken or dislodged.

Comfort:
warmth is akin to comfort. Clothe and shelter the victim
who will probably feel cold and clammy because of shock.
Insulate him from the cold ground. When bleeding is under
control reassure him because, humane considerations apart,
anxiety quickens the pulse and raises the blood pressure.

Pain:
makes a person restless, even when unconscious. Half-
measures are useless for severe pain; treat a fit adult with
full doses of morphine (D.1.4), provided he can breathe normally and has no head injury – when codeine (D.1.3) is the
drug of choice. Most chest injury victims breathe better after
pain relief. Narcotic analgesics give a pleasant feeling of
warmth and well-being.

Dress, pack, and bandage the wound; then splint it like a
fracture and leave it undisturbed.

Appearance of other sorts of bleeding

Bleeding commonly arises from wounds, but be aware of
hidden bleeding and the varied appearance of spilled blood.
For more detail on the conditions mentioned here refer to
appropriate chapters later in this book.

SALIVA

Bright red blood may trickle into the throat from a nose-bleed, bitten tongue, bleeding gums or tooth socket, injury to the nose, mouth or pharynx. It may be spat out, mixed with saliva either as streaks or lumps of clot, or swallowed Look carefully with a strong light for the source of bleeding, one being a fracture of the base of the skull, producing blood from the ears mixed with watery cerebro-spinal fluid.

SPUTUM

Pink flecks coughed up in frothy phlegm suggest blood from the lungs, possibly due to pneumonia, pulmonary oedema or embolus (fluid or clot in the lungs).

VOMIT

Swallowed blood irritates the stomach, causing vomiting. Peptic ulcer is a likely source of bright red fresh blood. Blood lying for more than a day in the stomach becomes partly digested and changes to dark brown like coffee grounds.

URINE

Scanty blood turns the urine cloudy or slightly orange; if profuse, a deep wine-red colour. If peeing causes burning pain look for infection. When the story tells of a blow in the flank, suspect bleeding from the kidney. If pain is acute, colicky, and extremely severe, think of a stone in the urinary passages.

STOOL

A little bright red blood streaked on the toilet paper suggests a crack at the anal margin caused by a small pile (haemor-rhoid), or by passing a constipated stool. Piles can bleed alarmingly, with clots. Digested blood (from an ulcer) that has passed the length of the gut produces, 6 to 8 hours later, a dark or tarry stool which can be confused with the black stool of someone taking iron tablets or some bismuth – containing over-the-counter antacids.

VAGINA

Normal menstrual rhythms are often interrupted by energetic activities, particularly on expeditions. A missed period suggests pregnancy, so in someone with vaginal bleeding consider miscarriage (abortion) or a ruptured ectopic pregnancy.

9

WOUNDS AND BITES

This chapter presumes a medical kit at least as comprehensive as that listed on pages 25–26. Improvising with imagination must supplement any missing items.

Superficial wounds

ABRASIONS

Grazes, scrapes, and minor burns need cleaning with copious water and soap; *dilution is the solution to pollution*. Superficial wounds heal best when left open to fresh air and allowed to dry and form a scab – nature's dressing. Avoid unctions that keep a wound moist; if infected, give an antibiotic by mouth rather than as ointment.

If the wound must be covered because of oozing, infection, or if the site is unsuitable for exposure, use a sterile gauze dressing secured with any sort of tape.

CUTS

Cover with a small sterile dressing (Band-Aid, Elastoplast). Close apposition of clean wound edges will give the least scar. Use sterile paper strips (Steri-strips) or 'butterfly dressings'. Paint tincture of benzoin on surrounding skin to make it tacky. Carefully place the strips, alternating the direction of pull of each, to bring the wound edges together and keep the tension equal down its length. For awkward places –

between the fingers, around the ankle – 'anchor dressings' conform closely to uneven contours.

BLISTERS

Blisters are usually caused by ill-fitting, stiff boots. Cover a sore 'hot-spot' immediately to prevent it rubbing and becoming a fluid-filled blister. Paint the surrounding skin with tincture of benzoin and apply tape – surgical, duct or moleskin – well above and below the rubbed area. To take the pressure off a large blister cut a doughnut from moleskin and place the hole over the bleb. Leave the tape in place for a week if necessary. Do not burst small blisters; if large and likely to burst from rubbing of a boot, clean the skin and puncture the edge using a needle sterilized by holding it in a flame till red-hot. Leave the overlying skin in place as a dressing. Clean with soap and water, and dress.

Deep wounds

LACERATIONS

Cleanse cut, torn, or mangled tissue and leave the wound agape to heal from the bottom. Close it later if necessary (delayed primary healing), as for war wounds. This is safer than trying to suture wounds in the wilds where sterility is impossible and because sutures themselves become a focus for infection, acting as foreign material in the wound. For this reason, though a simple enough procedure in itself, *there are no instructions in this book on how to suture*. Nature does a superb job with most wounds provided there is no infection; should she fail, a plastic surgeon can tidy up the scar much later.

PUNCTURE WOUNDS

Puncture wounds look tiny on the surface but may have a long track. Also there's no telling how deeply they penetrate, so beware – those of the chest and abdomen are potential minefields. Seek a surgeon quick.

GUNSHOT WOUNDS
Leave the bullet or pellets in place, unless easily extracted.

AMPUTATIONS
Stop bleeding, clean the amputated part and wrap it in dry sterile gauze. Place it in a plastic bag chilled by ice or snow (outside the bag), and accompany it and its owner to hospital. If only partially amputated, dress it in its most natural position. Pray that a surgeon may be able to sew the parts together again (18 hours is the maximum time for survival of an amputated part, properly chilled).

Bleeding (haemorrhage)

Severe external bleeding will almost always stop with firm pressure directly on the wound, raising the injured part and resting the victim. Deep internal haemorrhage is a more serious matter usually requiring surgery.

An average adult male has about 5½ litres of circulating blood, a female 4½ litres. Each can afford to lose about 1 litre before showing anaemia and shock. Loss of more than ⅓ of the total blood volume can kill. Children tolerate blood loss less well than adults. Severe bleeding, whether from arteries or veins (the difference is academic) must cease urgently.

Bleeding may halt spontaneously because muscle and elastic tissue in blood vessel walls contract; or shed blood forms fibrin clot in the wound (but rarely within an undamaged vessel); or hidden bleeding in a closed space either builds

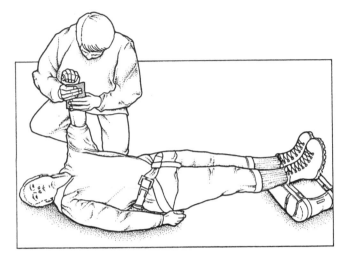

Stopping bleeding

up tension and closes off vessels in tissue planes between muscles, or bleeding continues unabated into the cavity.

Act: elevate the part above the level of the heart. Press steadily and firmly directly on a dressing of absorbent material placed well beyond the edges of the wound, and be prepared to keep up pressure for a long time. Most bleeding will stop eventually with pressure alone. A sterile dressing is preferable, but any reasonably clean material, especially if recently ironed, will suffice. Speed may prevent the victim dying of blood loss. A doctor can deal with any subsequent infection later.

Do not remove soaked dressings; just pack more on top. Clot forms around the mesh of fabric and seals small bleeding vessels and oozing capillaries. If clot is displaced bleeding will start again. Gel and colloid dressings dissolve in the wound and hasten clotting. Keep the wound packing in place by wrapping it with absorbent stretch crêpe bandage. This will splint the area and avoid movement that might restart bleeding. A wide, blind suture needle bite to close off the wound will be a focus for infection, and you may damage nerves and other structures in the depths of the wound – so don't.

Pressure points: don't waste valuable time searching for them.
Tourniquets: are potentially dangerous. They may obstruct veins without controlling arterial bleeding. If forgotten they will obstruct blood supply and cause gangrene of the limb beyond, pressure may damage nerves, and pain causes restlessness. If a tourniquet is necessary because other methods have failed to control bleeding (e.g. traumatic amputation of the hand), release the tourniquet every 45 minutes, mark a large T on the victim's forehead, and record on a label tied round his neck the time when it was applied. Rarely a large artery is severed and bleeding cannot be controlled by pressure or a tourniquet; you may have to clamp the ends with a haemostat and tie off the vessel with thread.

Cleaning:
rid the wound of grease and grime by washing with copious soap and water which gives bacteria less chance to survive and cause infection. Irrigate the depths of the wound forcefully using a 20ml syringe. Pick out dirt with forceps; do not scrub the wound because you will further damage tissue. Antiseptic solutions are no better than soap and water and can cause chemical irritation. The rescuer should work with hands washed as meticulously as the wound.

Dressings:
place a sterile dressing next to the wound; ironed cloth, unopened toilet paper or paper tissues, compressed wound

dressings or tightly packaged womens' sanitary towels. To increase the bulk of a dressing, slap on top any clean absorbent cloth, like a shirt.

Cover oozing wounds with paraffin gauze squares (Jelonet), or ones impregnated with antibiotic (Sofratulle). If a closed dressing is required, apply stretchy, clear plastic kitchen wrap straight onto a wound or a burn. Wrap a mangled limb temporarily in a plastic bag taped closed to the skin at both ends.

Function:
test for sensation and normal movement beyond the wound for tendon or nerve injury.

TETANUS PREVENTION

Anyone planning a trip should have a tetanus booster if more than 10 years since their last one. Within 3 days of a wound seek an anti-tetanus booster dose of 0.5–1.0ml, provided there is no history of previous reactions to anti-tetanus serum. (See page 256).

Infection

An infected wound looks red, swells, feels hot, and throbs painfully – especially if deep and dirty, or if caused by a puncture or bite. The body mobilizes white blood cells, which flow along dilated blood vessels into the inflamed area to combat bacteria. The resulting boil or abscess comprises pus made of gobbled-up bugs and dead tissue.

LOCALIZED INFECTION (BOIL OR ABSCESS)

A tense infected swelling usually comes to a head and forms a white or yellow boil with a soft centre of pus, which may burst on its own. A red streak of inflamed lymph channels may lead towards the heart; regional lymph nodes that drain the infected area swell – in the groin from the leg, in the armpit from the arm.

Act: heat encourages pus to gather. Soak the area in warm salt water or apply a hot compress of cloth dipped in boiling water and wrung out, every 6 hours. Honey, baking soda, or glycerine magnesium sulphate paste help draw out pus.

Where there's pus let it out. Lance an abscess with a soft centre to allow pus to drain. But beware of incising an abscess before it is 'ripe' because it will be painful and produce no pus. A quick stab into the stretched skin over a ripe abscess causes little pain especially if you apply ice or snow for 5 minutes beforehand. Incise deep and long so the hole will not seal over and nullify your good work of drainage. Sudden release of pus under pressure relieves pain instantly. Pack a deep hole with a wick of sterile gauze.

Treat: cephalosporin (D.2.1) as soon as a wound becomes red and inflamed. Avoid antibiotic ointments which may cause sensitivity reactions.

SPREADING INFECTION (CELLULITIS)
The skin around the wound looks red and angry, and feels hot and hard owing to swelling. Regional lymph nodes swell.

Act: immobilize the part and elevate it to reduce swelling.
Treat: antibiotics (D.2), in double dose, i/v if possible.

GENERALIZED INFECTION (BLOOD POISONING OR SEPTICAEMIA)
High fever and chills in the presence of infection suggest septicaemia – a serious complication needing urgent medical help.

Treat: antibiotics (D.2) i/v if possible, in double dose, and rest.

WOOD SPLINTER
Pull it out with forceps or tweezers; a difficult task even if judged to lie just under the skin. Inject 1ml of local anaesthetic xylocaine (D.17.1) directly into the area. Soak in hot

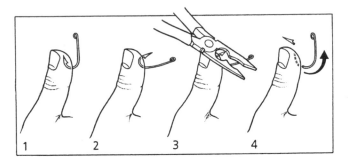

Removing fish-hook

water and try again but don't damage tissue by persevering. Left alone, pus will eventually form around a splinter and extrude it as pressure rises.

METAL FOREIGN BODY

Leave well alone unless easily removed with tweezers. A broken-off needle fragment may remain inert and harmless for years. Removing it surgically, even with X-ray help, is notoriously difficult.

FISH-HOOK

Push the hook onwards until it pierces the skin again. Cut off the barbed end with pliers (LM), cupping a hand over the cutters to prevent the barb flying into your own eye. Then withdraw the shank of the hook by the way it went in. If pliers are unavailable, hold the eye of the hook down against the skin, loop fishline or string around the hook, and jerk sharply along the plane of the skin surface thereby tearing it out.

BRUISES

Blood released under the skin breaks down in time, and the overlying skin turns to the colours of the rainbow.

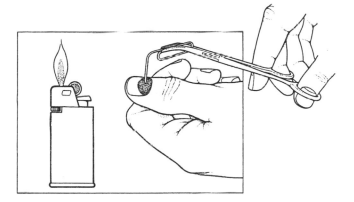

Draining fingernail

SUPERFICIAL BRUISES

Black eye:
blood collects in the loose tissues around the eye encircled
by the margin of the bony orbit. It will subside with ice and
time.

Fingernail blood blister (subungual haematoma):
a bash on a fingernail or a boulder dropped on a toe form
a tense, painful bruise at the root of the nail; it becomes
black, soggy on pressure and excruciatingly painful.
   Act: hold an opened metal paper clip in forceps or pliers
over a stove or a propane lighter flame (candle flame is not
hot enough). When the paper clip end is red-hot, push it
cautiously into the middle of the moon of the nail over the
bruise so it burns right through the nail but not into the nail
bed; the sizzling smells like a smithy. Old, dark blood spurts
out and the sun shines again from the face of the victim,

who will be your instant friend, unless you have plunged too deep. Alternatively, drill the base of the nail by rotating a penknife blade or a hypodermic needle.

Deep bruise (haematoma):
a painful swelling arises from blood pooled in muscle over the point of injury. Rest, elevation and ice may help it to subside. A tense bruise filled with fluid needs puncturing with the largest available needle to drain the pooled serum. Clean the skin carefully beforehand.

Bites

Wash any bite immediately with copious water and soap because mouths, including those of humans, are full of bacteria. Treat with an antibiotic any sign of infection – redness around the wound, or enlarged, tender neighbouring lymph glands. Check that the person's tetanus immunization is up-to-date; if not, he needs a booster dose soon.

Animal bites

RABIES
Rabies should be considered after an animal bite, especially in the tropics or in an endemic area. Although rare, rabies kills once it is manifest with painful spasms, especially on swallowing (causing hatred of water – hydrophobia), and excitement leading to convulsions and paralysis. Dogs are the commonest vectors, but foxes, the wolf family, skunks, racoons and bats can all carry rabies; rabbits, squirrels, chipmunks, rats and mice never do. Rabies virus lives in the saliva of an infected animal, affecting its nervous system and causing the frothing of mad dogs; the virus enters humans through a break in the skin, or possibly by spelunkers

breathing air in caves inhabited by rabid bats. Most domestic animals in the western world are immunized against rabies; not so in the tropics.

Prevention: if bitten or licked by a suspect animal, wash the wound liberally with soap and water and leave it open to the sun because ultraviolet light kills some viruses. Cage any suspect animal; if not possible, shoot it. If the animal is alive and free of rabies after 10 days, the victim of the bite is safe; if it develops signs of rabies kill it and send the head, carefully wrapped, to a laboratory for examination of the brain. If the result is positive for rabies, or immediately after the bite of a known rabid animal, start a course of anti-rabies vaccine.

Treat: rabies immune globulin (RIG) 20 IU/kg in one dose as soon as possible after exposure + human diploid cell vaccine (HDCV) 1ml i/m at different sites for prevention on Days 0, 7, 28; for treatment on Days 0, 3, 7, 14, 30 & 90.

TULARAEMIA

This is caused by handling diseased or dead rabbits and beavers, the organism is inoculated by thorns and briars leading to ulcers and enlarged lymph glands. Seek medical advice.

Snakebites

Less than 1 in 20 persons bitten by snakes die from snakebite poisoning. North America has pit vipers (rattlesnakes, cotton-mouths, copperheads), and coral snakes. Viper venom can cause immediate painful stinging inflammation at the bite site, and tissue sloughing. Occasionally a severe body reaction occurs with shock, chills, vomiting and convulsions. Breathing and kidney failure follow. Coral snakes rarely bite but if they do the reaction may be delayed 12 hours, when the victim suddenly collapses. Cobras are only one of the many deadly snakes which abound in the tropics, so consult an appropriate book.

In a snake area wear boots, carry a stick and a flashlight at night, and examine clothes, footwear and sleeping bag before climbing in. Snakes only attack when frightened or provoked. If possible, kill the snake without damaging identifying marks around the head; pick up the head cautiously because it can strike up to an hour after being cut off. Take the snake's head and the victim to the local hospital, which may keep anti-venom against the local varieties of poisonous snakes.

Act: wash the bite thoroughly with soap and water. Do not suck or slash the skin over the bite, or pee on it. Bandage firmly and tightly over the bite around the entire limb, splint it, and keep it dependent to reduce venom entering the blood-stream. Do not freeze or use tourniquets, which can lead to gangrene of the limb. If cobra venom has been spat into the eyes irrigate them thoroughly.

Treat: antivenom 50 to 400ml immediately, depending on the severity of the poison. Be sure the victim has actually been bitten because horse serum, from which the antivenom is made, can cause grave hypersensitivity reactions and ana-phylactic shock. Treat pain and give reassurance because a snakebite strikes terror into the heart. Give a tetanus booster if not up-to-date. Do not use antibiotics unless infection follows.

SCORPIONS, SPIDERS, CATERPILLARS, CENTIPEDES AND OTHER CREEPIE-CRAWLIES

Bites may be venomous causing symptoms varying from local pain to shock and collapse. Spray DEET (diethyltolua-mide) or permethrin in places like outhouse seats where the beasties may lurk and give a nasty bite.

Treat: similar to snakebite. Antivenom is available against scorpions and spiders (black widow). Local anaesthetic injected into the site may ease the pain.

Insect bites

BEES, WASPS AND HORNETS

Stings can be painful and unpleasant. They can also kill a sensitive or allergic person by anaphylaxis, a reaction which causes giant welts (urticaria), severe wheezing, tight chest, stridorous choking and shock. Allergic people should be skin tested; if positive with a history of a previous severe reaction, they need venom desensitizing injections (which may themselves cause a grave allergic reaction) every 4 weeks indefinitely during the season. They should wear a Medic-Alert medallion and carry a kit containing 2 ampoules of adrenaline 0.3ml of 1:1,000 solution in pre-loaded syringes with a needle attached (Epi Pen).

Act: remove the sting with tweezers. Apply a hot compress. Neutralize the venom; bee venom is acid so apply bicarbonate of soda or weak ammonia; wasp venom is alkaline so use vinegar or lemon juice. Antihistamines (D.3) ease the itch.

Treat: adrenaline (D.7.2) 1:1,000, 0.3ml i/v (slowly), s/c, or i/m for severe allergy or anaphylaxis; if in severe shock, repeated every ½ hour. Beware! adrenaline can cause the pulse to race and beat irregularly.

MOSQUITOS AND BLACK FLIES

Mosquitos are described under malaria (see page 259). Black flies and 'no-see-ums' thrive in the sub-arctic. They penetrate mosquito netting and give a vicious bite out of proportion to their tiny size. Danger comes from infection of the bites because of wild scratching.

SCABIES, LICE, NITS, FLEAS AND BED BUGS

Scabies mites burrow under the skin of the trunk and limbs (everywhere excluding the face) causing intense itching, worse at night in a warm bed. Tiny red spots are visible at the bite, and scratch marks are everywhere. Lice (pediculus) lay eggs (nits), which are cemented to the hair of the head and pubis, and in clothing seams. Fleas cause intense itching and leave a trail of bites around the midriff. Bed bugs bite and smell, but do not carry disease.

Treat: [permethrin] for scabies; apply one thin layer of the lotion all over the body excluding the head, leave it for 24 hours, then shower. Repeat once in a week if necessary, or use [benzyl benzoate] nightly for 3 nights. Hot wash all clothes and bedding, air sleeping bags in the sun, and treat the family or tentmates likewise. For lice do a single shampoo of one tablespoonful for 4 minutes, then rinse and dry. For scabies and lice, treat all contacts.

LEECHES AND TICKS

Leeches are troublesome in rain forests and tropical marshes. The first sign may be a bootful of blood at the end of the day because bites are painless and prevent blood clotting. Leeches find their way into laced boots, so open sandals have the advantage that you can see them early and deal with them. A flick of a finger, a touch of salt, a lighted cigarette or tincture of iodine makes a leech drop off; do not pull the body or the head will be left in the wound and continue to irritate. Clean the wound with soap and water, and press to stop bleeding.

JELLYFISH, STING RAYS, SEA ANEMONES

Stings from these sea creatures cause intense burning pain, local swelling and red weals. Sometimes the victim is prostrated.

Treat: as for other bites.

Itching

Itching can drive a person crazy, literally; more scratch, more itch. Dirty finger nails will turn a bite septic.

Treat: calamine lotion (D.11.4) soothes and cools more than cream; make starch or oatmeal paste by adding 1 cup to 1 litre of boiling water and apply the cooled paste to the area.

Antihistamines quell itching (promethazine (D.3.1) but cause drowsiness; (chlorpheniramine (D.3.2) is the least soporific). Antihistamine creams can sensitize the skin to oral antihistamines taken later and a violent skin reaction may result. Only use betamethasone (D.11.1) steroid cream if other methods fail.

INSECT REPELLENTS

Applied to the skin, they repel insects for 4 hours maximum.

Treat: an insect repellent containing [DEET (diethyltoluamide) or permethrin].

INSECTICIDES

The clothing and the person wearing it must be treated; crystals of powder or droplets of spray stick to the insect and slowly paralyse it.

10

BURNS AND HEAT INJURY

Burns are assessed by measuring the burned body surface area (bsa) (see page 121).

Minor burns (less than 15% bsa) usually heal unaided.

Major burns (more than 15% bsa in adults, 10% in children) threaten life with consequences stretching far beyond the burn wound itself.

Minor burns

SUNBURN

Sunburn is a painful nuisance, especially for those with fair skin, red hair or freckles. Sun reflects strongly off water, sand and snow – an effect enhanced by wind. Ultraviolet rays penetrate hazy clouds stealthily, the higher the altitude the more they burn, and each 300m altitude rise adds 4% to the intensity. Avoid sunburn by rationing sunlight on the skin with adequate clothing; wear a wide-brimmed hat or peaked cap with neck cover, and sun-glasses with blinker side-pieces and nose-shields (beware the underside of lip and nose). Falling asleep in the sun is a sure way to burn, and even a sola topi won't save mad dogs or Englishmen at midday.

Sun creams and lotions screen the burning parts of the ultraviolet spectrum, but with excessive sun they just act as fat for frying; none speed 'le bronzage'. The Sun Protection

Factor (SPF) should be marked on the bottle; the higher the number, the more the protection – #15 is for average use. Para-aminobenzoic acid (PABA) is the commonest active ingredient, but this can cause allergy; if so, use zinc oxide, an opaque screen.

Act: find shade if skin goes shrimp-pink and feels prickly and hot. Baking soda compresses or calamine soothe badly burned lobster-red skin, which will blister. Watch for severe general body upset (hypothermia see page 220) with headache, vomiting and fainting; fan and cool with ice.

Treat: antihistamine (D.3) allays itching; paracetamol (D.1.1) for fever; betamethasone steroid cream (D.11.1) relieves bad burns. Avoid topical local anaesthetic and antihistamine creams which can cause sensitivity reactions.

FLAME BURNS

Open air:
flame burns and scalds go hand-in-hand with hot cooking pans, boiling water, and hot fat. The flash of flame from ignited gasoline or propane passes in a second; the skin turns brown or black, but if the burn is only superficial it will heal within a couple of weeks. Flaming clothing continues to burn the skin for several seconds, often causing a deep burn which takes weeks, or months, to heal and may need skin-grafting. Some synthetic fabrics like nylon and polypropylene melt and burn deeply; fireproof synthetic materials are labelled as such. Wool and natural fibre do not hold flame, so the burn is delayed in reaching the skin; but wool keeps boiling water in contact with the skin, prolonging the scalding time. Boiling water and frying pan fat aflame on bare skin often burn deeply.

Enclosed space:
explosions within an enclosed space (e.g. a tent, snow cave, or camper van) produce hot gases; if inhaled, they burn the

air passages and lungs – often fatally. Liquid propane gas is heavier than air and, when spilled, settles on the floor and explodes if ignited by a flame or a spark.

FRICTION BURNS

Deep friction rope burns to the hands, neck and back can occur when a climber tries to hold a falling companion, or when roping down.

ELECTRICAL BURNS

Deeper and more extensive than at first sight, electrical burns heal slowly, especially at the point where the current entered and left the body.

LIGHTNING BURNS

with a direct strike the burn makes a fern-like pattern spreading over the skin surface; an indirect burn is caused by superheated air near the object struck. The electric discharge of lightning during a thunderstorm produces about 30,000,000 volts and 250,000 amps, but is very short-lasting (1–100 milliseconds). Lightning kills by stopping the heart and breathing; external injury and burns are uncommon.

Prevention:
during a thunderstorm, shelter in a stone or brick building or a car (the metal body affords protection, not the rubber tires). Avoid tents because poles and wet fabric act as conductor rods. Groups must scatter, each person staying well apart. Crouch to avoid being the highest object around, sit on a rope or sleeping pad for insulation, and put down ice axes or other metal conductors. Flee mountain summits, hilltops, ridges and rock walls (stay 3m away). In forest, stay in thick bush and avoid isolated tall trees.

TYPES OF LIGHTNING INJURY

One third of all people struck die; others recover spontaneously and begin breathing within seconds.

Head and neck:
lightning may enter by the eyes (cataracts, blindness) or ears (drum or mastoid rupture, deafness). Victims will probably lose consciousness and then be confused after recovery.

Skin:
deep burns are rare. Superficial steam burns occur in moist areas in linear, rosette-like, or feathery patterns. Clothing may be blasted apart and shredded.

Feet:
if the person is standing the energy may flow up one leg and down the other, literally 'blowing their shoes and socks off'.

Extremities:
intense spasm of blood vessels causes blue mottled limbs.

Blunt injury:
intense generalized contraction of muscles may throw the person to the ground, fracturing bones or causing internal injury.

Act: if still breathing and moaning the person will probably recover; if the heart stops the outlook is poor. Evacuate him quickly. Don't be afraid to touch lightning victims; they never store electrical charge that can affect the rescuer.

Car Battery:
when booster cables are connected wrongly a battery may explode violently, especially if a spark ignites escaping hydrogen gas.

Act (minor burns): cool immediately with cold water or snow to reduce burning time and to relieve pain. Wash with copious water and leave open to the air to dry; if not feasible, cover with a small sterile dressing. The burn usually heals quickly and completely, provided there is no infection.

Major burns

Major burns cause tissue damage and fluid loss; together these lead to 'burn shock' similar to the clinical shock that follows severe bleeding (see page 101). Emotional shock – fear, pain, and fainting – that follows the burning accident compounds and worsens clinical shock. Major burns *always* need fluid replacement.

Tissue damage

A burn is a wound; its severity depends on its depth, extent and location, which together determine the time a wound will take to heal, and whether skin-grafting will be necessary.

DEPTH OF BURN

Partial-thickness (superficial):
the burn penetrates to, and harms to a variable extent, the germinal layer from where cells spread out to form new skin. If kept clean and dry, partial-thickness burns usually heal unaided in 7–21 days. Infection delays healing and may convert a partial-thickness burn to full-thickness. (N.B. the classification first, second, or third degree is unhelpful).

Full-thickness (deep):
the burn extends through the germinal layer destroying

nerves and blood vessels, hair follicles and sweat glands which lie in that layer. The skin will not regenerate on its own and usually requires skin-grafting. The colour of burned skin is a poor guide to burn depth; better tests are:
– pinprick: if the person can feel the prick of a sterile needle firm enough to draw blood (light touch is not enough) the burn is superficial (a full-thickness burn destroys nerves, so pain is absent).
– pressure: deeply burned skin feels leathery and firm on pressure – a useful test in scalds where the skin looks pink. If colour returns quickly on removing pressure the burn is superficial.

Act: before focusing attention on the victim's burn wound, attend to his airway and treat pain.

Airway:
for a burn victim to die from airway block is an avoidable tragedy.

> Endotracheal intubation should occur early rather than late. A tracheotomy may be needed on reaching hospital – never in the field.

Pain:
not only is pain unpleasant but also it aggravates shock. Reassure the victim and give enough drugs to kill his pain. A superficial burn will usually hurt because nerve-endings in the epidermis remain intact; they are destroyed in a deep burn which may be painless.

Treat: morphine (D.1.4).

Managing a major burn in the wilds will be very difficult. The *ideal treatment* is explained here, yet I understand your limitations. Do not despair just because you are in remote country several days or weeks away from help. Ingenuity and common sense must prevail.

THE BURN WOUND

Whatever the cause and degree, the immediate care of the burn wound is the same; refinements in treatment come later. All treatment is aimed towards keeping the burn wound clean and avoiding infection.

Cool:
immediately douse any burn, whatever the cause, with cold water or snow for at least 10 minutes. Cooling halts burning and eases pain.

Undress:
remove clothing to examine the full extent of the burn. Leave in place charred fabric stuck to the skin because pulling it away may restart bleeding; it will be sterile anyway from the heat. Remove rings and jewellery before swelling occurs.

Wash:
with copious soap and water. With sterile forceps remove dead tissue that comes away easily. Irrigate chemical burns (especially lime in the eyes) with plain water for at least 10 minutes.

Record:
draw a careful diagram of the area of the burn according to the rule of 9s (see diag.), and the depth of burning (pinprick test) in order to follow the progress of healing during the long days ahead. Ask how the accident occurred and what steps were taken to extinguish the cause of the burn.

Open air exposure:
provided it remains absolutely clean of infection, a burn wound exposed to open air will form a crusting scab (eschar or carapace) under which healing goes on free from bacteria. Eventually the scar separates leaving a raw area (granulation

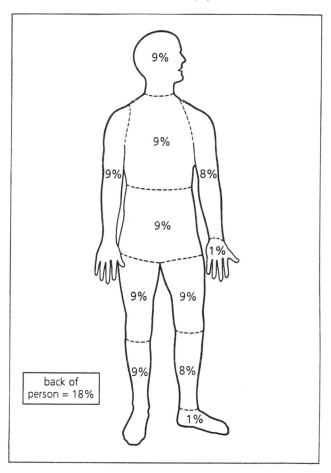

Rule of 9s

tissue). In wilderness open exposure will be nigh impossible and dressing will be needed.

Dressing:
cover the wound with clean, sterile, dry linen or non-stick dressing. A dressing acts as a mechanical barrier to infection and absorbs exudate from the wound, allowing it to dry. Place 2 layers of plain paraffin gauze next to the burn. Extend the dressing at least a hand's breadth beyond the edge of the burn. Apply a pad of absorbent cotton on top of the dressing to soak up exuded fluid. Finally, wrap a crêpe bandage evenly over the dressing, firmly enough to keep it in place but not so tight as to restrict circulation. Do not smear the burn with butter, burn creams, or patent potions which confuse the picture and make dressings stick fast. Avoid antibiotic creams which encourage the growth of resistant bacteria.

If there is no immediate chance of reaching help, a burn dressing can remain in place for up to a week provided it remains dry and free of infection. Repeated peeking at the wound lays open a path for infection. As soon as plasma soaks through the dressing, replace the outer absorbent packing only, leaving the immediate dressing in place. If it smells foul, has a pussy discharge, if pain and redness develop in skin away from the burn, or if the victim's temperature rises, undo the dressing completely and start again because these are signs of infection.

Blisters:
leave a small blister alone and use a moleskin doughnut to keep off pressure while it heals. Leave large blisters intact if possible as they form a skin roof and a good sterile enclosure. If the blister rubs it will break anyway, so puncture the blebs with a sterile needle or blade. Careful lancing on the first day can be quite painless. Keep the resulting open wound scrupulously clean as infection can easily creep in.

Blisters that break by themselves and become infected are very painful.

Treat: antibiotic (D.2) for at least 10 days if infection supervenes.

Codeine (D.1.3) or morphine (D.1.4). Dressing changes are agony, so give a strong pain-killer before starting

Tetanus toxoid; get a booster dose as soon as possible (see page 104).

Skin grafting.
If the wound is clean early skin grafting of a full-thickness burn can be done soon after arrival in hospital and can prevent hideous disabling deformities.

Fluid loss

Capillaries damaged by burning leak plasma (or serum), the fluid portion of blood, which exudes from the raw surface, form blisters, and collect in swollen tissues. The body compensates by shifting blood from skin and gut to pool in the central circulation, and by compulsive thirst and drinking which make up for some of the lost fluid – early signs of 'burn shock'.

Replace plasma quickly (if possible i/v) to avoid shock after a major burn; the longer the delay the worse the outcome. 'Burn shock' develops slowly over several hours owing to accumulated toxic products of tissue destruction and plasma loss, compared to severe bleeding which causes immediate shock in proportion to blood loss. The victim appears deceptively well soon after the accident but then deteriorates over the next 24 to 36 hours. Some red cells are destroyed in the scorched skin leading to anaemia, others pass into the circulation and fragment, later lodging in the kidney and giving the urine a red-brown colour.

Act: replace fluid according to your estimate of the victim's needs based on measuring the burned *area* accurately according to the rule of 9s; disregard the *depth* of burning for fluid replacement.

Restoring fluid balance after a major burn is best done by i/v drip; in the boondocks you must consider other routes which, though they cannot overload the circulation, are less efficient.

Fluid needs are: 4 to 5ml × body weight (kg) × % burn area each 24 hours at a rate of ½ the volume in the first 8 hour period, ¼ in each of the next 8 hour periods (plasma needs about ½ the volume). The timing is calculated from the time of the burn and therefore initial fluid replacement must catch up and may have to be given rapidly. Thereafter give enough fluid to produce 30–50ml of urine each hour.

ORAL

The person should drink 3 litres daily if possible, taking small sips rather than big gulps to avoid vomiting. Plain water will do, but the WHO formula (D.18) may replace enough electrolyte, glucose, and water to keep the victim of a 50% burn alive.

RECTAL

Insert a greased wide-bore tube as high up the rectum as possible, preferably about 15cm (7") from the anus. Run in fluid of any sort as fast as the victim can retain it without overflow.

NASO-GASTRIC

If the person cannot drink, pass a greased 14mm diameter naso-gastric tube into the stomach via the nose (difficult sometimes to turn the bend at the back of the pharynx), or through the mouth (he may gag and vomit). When the tube is in the stomach, fluid in an attached funnel will start to flow; listen for gurgling with an ear or stethoscope laid against the upper abdomen.

SUBCUTANEOUS

Insert the needle of an i/v apparatus under the loose skin of the abdomen, or just above the clavicle. The needle must lie in the plane between skin and muscle where fluid can spread and be absorbed slowly – 3 litres in each 24 hours.

INTRAVENOUS FLUID

Choose a large vein as the i/v drip may have to last several days. Preferably use human plasma reconstituted with sterile water which contains all the essential proteins; Ringer's lactate or normal saline will do temporarily.

Special burn sites

FACE, EYELIDS, EYES

Expose most face burns to fresh air. If lax tissues of the lids swell and close the person's eyes, reassure him that he is not going blind. Burns of the window of the eye (cornea) are uncommon because blinking usually occurs instantly. Wash out corrosive chemicals with water until every particle has gone. Lids may retract as the burn dries leaving the cornea exposed and liable to ulcerate. Snow blindness follows an ultraviolet burn of the cornea.

Treat: chloramphenicol ointment (D.12.1) into the eye twice daily to lubricate the lids and stave off infection; 2% homatropine drops (D.12.3) twice daily to keep the pupil dilated and ease painful spasm of the iris. Use dark glasses rather than an eye pad, which when soggy from tears is uncomfortable and harbours bugs.

If lips, tongue or nostril hairs are scorched after an explosion, the victim will probably have inhaled burning gas; his prospects are poor. The larynx and trachea swell making the voice husky at first, followed by croaking from a blocked airway. A lung burn usually leads to pneumonia, and ultimately to breathing failure and death.

CHEST AND NECK

If the burn is circumferential a crust, like a breast-plate of armour, may form and restrict breathing.

Make longitudinal cuts through the full thickness of burned skin to relieve breathing (see below – escharotomy).

HANDS

Nasty contracture deformities form unless the burned hands are kept moving while healing. Cover the whole hand liberally with antibiotic cream and put it in a plastic bag taped at the wrist. Encourage the victim to exercise his fingers continually to prevent the skin hardening and the fingers becoming stiff. Elevate the hand to reduce swelling. With a bagged hand the victim can do a lot for himself without pain; a mitten over the top protects the bag and looks less distasteful.

Deep burns of the circumference of limbs or fingers harden and the scab may contract like a ring and cut off the blood supply or restrict movement. Check by pin-prick for pain sensation; if absent, consider escharotomy.

ESCHAROTOMY

This seemingly drastic, though simple, surgical procedure may be limb-saving. Make a deep knife cut through a tight constricting band of charred skin along the lateral sides of the limb or digits. The wound will spread owing to the pressure within. To be effective the cut must extend beyond the top and bottom of the eschar down into the unburned zone, which feels pain and may bleed. If the cuts are adequate, the swollen veins and mottled blue colour of the skin return to a healthy pink. When fingers are burned deeply to the tips all round, escharotomy is unlikely to help.

Finally, do not delay evacuating the burned victim to hospital; he will travel best immediately after the accident, before shock sets in. Do the best you can in the time while waiting for rescue. Reassure him that you are doing everything possible to reach help urgently. Do not brush off his questions, but give a realistic reply. Let's hope optimism is warranted.

Heat injury

Normally heat loss balances heat gain to keep the body temperature within narrow limits, this being regulated by a thermostat within the brain. The body gains heat from its own basal metabolism, by exercise, and from the environment. It loses heat mainly by evaporation through sweating, also by conduction and convection both of which are blocked by high heat and humidity. Exercise increases heat gain tenfold; in hot climates heat gain may exceed heat loss causing core temperature to rise, sometimes to dangerous levels. Heat illness is most likely in the young and old; in humid, hot climates; and in occupations that demand extreme exertion.

Acclimatization to heat takes 3–10 days and is stimulated by an hour of exercise a day in the heat.

Prevention:
avoid heavy exercise in high temperatures and high humidity but, if unavoidable, drink water before you feel thirsty and continue after feeling satisfied – every hour, and enough to produce clear urine regularly (12–20 litres daily). Avoid fancy electrolyte and sugar sports drinks during activity because they slow absorption of water from the bowel.

However, replace salt later or heat cramps may follow. Wear light-coloured, loose-fitting clothes that cover all sun-exposed skin. Eschew alcohol and caffeine, both diuretics that make you pee.

HEAT EXHAUSTION

Heat exhaustion develops over hours or days owing to water and salt loss; it can occur even at modest air temperatures, 16°C (60°F), if thirst does not stimulate adequate drinking to replace fluid after vigorous exercise. Ideal conditions for heat exhaustion are a hot day, bright sun, high humidity, calm wind and too much clothing.

Look:
rectal temperature is normal, or moderately raised, 39°C (102°F) to 41°C (105°F); thirst and profuse sweating; goose-flesh and chills; headache, nausea, dizziness and weakness; rapid pulse. He may become mentally strange, convulse and fall unconscious, progressing to heatstroke.

Act: rest the victim in the shade; wet him to increase evaporation; give copious water by mouth.

HEATSTROKE

Heatstroke can kill. The brain is deranged by raised body temperature brought on by vigorous exercise in high humidity even with a relatively low air temperature. Heart, liver and kidneys also suffer, worse with high fever and dehydration, and in the elderly.

Look:
rectal temperature is above 41°C (106°F), but do not diagnose heatstroke by temperature alone. Without warning the person may become drowsy, irritable and unsteady; then confused, delirious and comatose. The skin is still sweaty when he collapses but may become hot and dry 1 to 2 hours afterwards because of damage to sweat glands.

Act: immediate, rapid and thorough cooling can save a life. Fan wet skin to increase evaporation, or rub ice or snow vigorously on the neck, abdomen, axillae and groins. Immerse the trunk in a stream, but not the limbs because peripheral vessels will constrict, reducing heat loss.

Stop cooling only when the rectal temperature is 39°C (102°F) or when he improves mentally. Watch to see it does not rise again. Painful shivering may need analgesics.

Treat: 1 litre of 5% dextrose saline i/v over 30 minutes, or as much as he can tolerate by mouth.

HEAT CRAMPS

occur in fatigued muscles of persons who sweat and drink fluid without replacing salt.

HEAT FAINT

after standing erect and still (e.g. soldiers on parade), because calf muscles are static causing blood to pool in the periphery and deprive the brain.

11

LIMB INJURY

Soft tissue injuries

Injuries to muscles, tendons, and ligaments are important far exceeding their severity, because they hamper the escape to safety of a person injured in the mountains.

BRUISES AND CONTUSIONS

Muscle haematoma:
a blood vessel broken by a blunt blow to muscle (e.g. in thigh or buttock) can leak a litre of blood into surrounding soft tissues. The tense, painful swelling (haematoma) formed may take weeks to subside.

Act: plunge a wide-bore needle into the centre, if soft, after carefully cleaning the skin. If you strike gold, a fluid of that colour will flow out – serum from broken down blood cells.

Subperiosteal haematoma:
a blow on a bone near the skin surface (e.g. on the front of the shin) may cause bleeding under the periosteum, a thin membrane that enwraps bone and under which run nerves and blood vessels. The pooled blood-bruise stretches the periosteum, causing much pain and tenderness. Subperiosteal haematomas rarely need to be drained because less blood collects than in loose muscle tissue.

Act: rest, elevation and ice quell further bleeding and reduce swelling.

SPRAINS AND STRAINS

Ligaments and muscles may stretch or tear when a joint is bent beyond its normal range of movement, yet the bones remain intact. A sprain swells immediately (usually round a joint), hurts and is tender; lack of deformity distinguishes it from a displaced fracture or a dislocation. If the joint can be stressed past its normal limits, a ligament tear is likely. Severe sprains – commonly ankles, knees, and thumbs   are as crippling in the outdoors as fractures, and can take as long, or longer, to heal.

Act: cool the part with ice, snow or stream water for 15 minutes in each hour, elevate the limb above body level to reduce swelling and relieve pain. Support the joint firmly with tape or elastic bandage.

TEARS

Knee and ankle ligaments, Achilles and biceps tendons, and knee cartilages are commonly torn.

Act: immobilize by splinting; surgical repair may need to follow later.

TENDINITIS, BURSITIS, ARTHRITIS

Inflammation of a tendon, bursa (a fluid-filled cushion beneath a tendon) or a joint is painful and incapacitating because the underlying joint becomes stiff. Examples are shoulder (subacromial bursitis), elbow (epicondylitis), hip (trochanteric bursitis) and heel (Achilles tendinitis).

Act: rest, elevate, ice.

Treat: paracetamol (D.1.1) relieves pain and ibuprofen (D.1.2) reduces inflammation.

VEINS

Rupture by blunt injury will cause a haematoma (e.g. long saphenous vein). Inflammation causes thrombo-phlebitis.

SUPERFICIAL THROMBO-PHLEBITIS

A vein becomes tender, hardened into a cord, and the overlying skin turns red (e.g. varicose veins of the leg; forearm veins after i/v injection).

DEEP THROMBO-PHLEBITIS

Deep veins of the legs can become inflamed and clot (thrombosis), particularly in climbers lying around stormbound at altitude and not drinking enough. Viscous, treacly blood is liable to clot, forming a pulmonary embolus – a very serious matter (see below). Pain arises deep in the calf; feet and ankles swell. Pushing on the ball of the foot to bring the big toe nearer the kneecap causes pain deep in the calf (Homan's sign). The temperature is raised.

Act: rest with legs elevated and bandaged from groin to ankle until at least 3 days after all pain has subsided. Then evacuate urgently.

PULMONARY EMBOLUS

Clot from a deep vein thrombosis in the calf can detach forming an embolus which traverses the heart, coming to rest in the lungs. A big embolus can kill, owing to massive right heart failure; in a less severe case the victim is shocked, breathless, and cyanosed. Sudden pain in the chest may mimic a heart attack. Cough produces blood-stained, often frothy, sputum; deep breathing hurts.

CEREBRAL EMBOLUS

A 'stroke' weakens, or paralyses, one side of the face or the body.

Bone injuries

JOINT DISLOCATION

Dislocation occurs when one bone in a joint is displaced. The signs are similar to a fracture – swelling, deformity, pain, loss of use – but the diagnosis is usually obvious from the abnormal position of the joint compared with its uninjured opposite.

Act: attempt to reduce a dislocation like a fracture. Often easily done immediately, but if left a few minutes the overlying muscles go into spasm which nothing short of a general anaesthetic will relax. Nerves and blood vessels lie close to joints, so always feel for pulses before trying to reduce a dislocation. Surrounding ligaments and soft tissues may be torn. Take courage and try to reduce a dislocation that may allow a crippled person to help himself and others retreat safely.

Treat: morphine (D.1.4); before attempting reduction, pull firmly and steadily (traction) in the axis of the limb while an assistant pulls in the opposite direction (see specific dislocations).

FRACTURE

Fracture = break, no more no less; but a fractured femur sounds more dramatic than a broken thigh. Just as a chair leg will break if you knock, bend, twist, pull or crush it beyond certain limits, so will bones break or crack. Bones mend in the same way as wounds heal. Bone is a plastic, living framework wrapped in a tough membrane of periosteum to which muscles, tendons and ligaments are attached. Periosteum is rich in nerve fibres and registers most of the pain of a broken bone.

Closed and open fractures:
the distinction is important in practical care. Skin overlying

a closed fracture is intact; in an open fracture it is breached from within by jagged bone ends, or by force from outside. Underlying fractured bone is open to infection, which delays healing, smoulders and may progress to deep infection of bone (osteomyelitis) – a dreaded complication.

All fractures need splinting to prevent movement of the broken fragments which causes pain and further damage to neighbouring muscles, nerves and blood vessels. Stable (immobile) fractures may become unstable if inadequately supported.

Ask: how did the accident happen, did the victim hear the crack of breaking bone, where is the pain, can he move the part himself?

Look: compare the injured side with its uninjured normal opposite side; to inspect the injury remove clothing, if necessary by cutting along seams. Swelling or deformity (angulation) will become obvious at a glance.

Feel: begin away from the area of pain and gradually work towards the limb. Watch the victim's face constantly for a flicker of pain; you will learn nothing by staring at your own hands. To hurt a patient is inexcusable, and many medical students thereby have failed their final exams.

SHOCK (from fractures) (see chapter 8)

The victim may be emotionally shocked because of severe pain or anxiety about the outcome of the accident, a forced bivouac or a rescue call-out. He may also be in physiological shock from loss of blood into the tissues causing diminished blood volume, low blood pressure and rapid pulse. A badly fractured femur may release a litre of blood into soft tissue around the bone ($= \frac{1}{5}$ of the total blood volume). Bleeding arises from the bone marrow cavity, vessels in the periosteum and surrounding muscle, and tissues torn by the jagged bone ends. With multiple fractures and open wounds blood loss may be fatal.

Signs and symptoms of fractures

Pain:
most fractures cause a dull ache; they become excruciatingly painful when bone ends grate, or periosteum stretches. Tenderness is invariable, and gentle pressure over even a small break causes pain, which worsens shock.

Swelling:
hidden bleeding and oedema fluid cause swelling, reduced by rest, elevation and ice. Bruising appears later as blood seeps through to the skin.

Open wounds need special cleaning before splinting to avoid infection. Clear away dirt and debris, and wash the wound with copious water and soap; cover with a bulky sterile dressing, firmly taped.

Treat: broad-spectrum antibiotic (D.2) and tetanus toxoid as soon as possible.

Deformity:
correct severe angular deformity early, before swelling and muscle spasm develop; this is safe and harmless if done without undue resistance from, or pain to, the victim. Go ahead:
– if you have the expertise and confidence, knowing it will take many days to reach help
– if the bone is markedly malaligned and in peril of stretching or pinching nerves or blood vessels (check for the return of an absent pulse after straightening)
– if the skin is taut and blanched, suggesting compromised blood supply from pressure within.

Loss of use:
the victim will hold the injured part quite still, guarding it from pain – nature's splinting. Pain and instability discourage movement, so loss of use suggests fracture.

Associated damage:
damage to soft tissues around the fracture may be worse than the bone injury itself.
– *blood vessels:* tear and bleed. Pinching an artery in the fracture, or spasm resulting from irritation by a broken bone, restricts circulation to the whole limb. Tissues around a fracture swell and hamper blood flow.
– *skin:* is weakened by swelling, stretching and bruising. Broken skin converts a closed fracture into an open one. Warm, pink skin beyond the injury suggests adequate blood flow. Beware of blue or white skin that remains blanched on pressure, or if the pulse is absent.
– *nerves:* may be damaged, causing numbness, loss of pain and sensation, and paralysis.
  Act: if the person is merely severely bruised or suffering a sprain, he may be able to continue unaided after firm taping. With a suspected fracture loosen tight clothing and avoid bandages that restrict circulation. Once an unstable bone is immobilized by splinting the victim can be handled with less pain and damage. Complete immobilization is possible only in a plaster cast.

Reducing a fracture:
before trying to reduce a fracture explain to the person what you intend to do so he will be as relaxed as possible.
  Treat: morphine (D.1.4); a nip of brandy may soothe the victim, but alcohol is not a pain-killer.
  Have two people pull steadily in opposite directions to exert traction. Take a firm grasp on uninjured skin well away from the fracture and gently pull on the limb for 3 to 5 minutes

to overcome muscle spasm; a helper holds the limb near the trunk, pulling opposite. Handle the limb 'in one piece' so the bone ends do not grate. Sudden painful movement, especially in a muscular victim, will cause overlying muscles to lock firmly in spasm, cancelling any chance of reducing the fracture. Traction usually removes pain; so keep pulling before attempting to reduce the fracture. It also improves circulation and nerve function across the fracture site.

Reduce the fracture by increasing traction gently, firmly, resolutely and without hurry. Watch the victim's face all the time to ensure you are not hurting him unnecessarily. Once the bone ends are separated, pain disappears and it is easier to restore them to their natural position ready for splinting. But do not relax traction until the limb is splinted. Do not persist in hurting the victim by seeking perfect alignment. Aim to get the bone roughly straight; an orthopaedic surgeon can tidy up any angulation problems later.

Splinting:
splint a fracture to immobilise the joint above and below the injury. Delay splinting if being trussed up in an awkward situation means the victim cannot help in his own evacuation to a safer place. If he has to be carried on a stretcher, pad below weight-bearing points (e.g. heels) and between bony prominences (e.g. ankles) using spare clothing or a ring pad like a doughnut. Fill hollows under the knees. Tie splinting bandages firmly but not so tight as to impede circulation. Leave toes and fingers open to view so you can observe their colour and temperature; if they become pale, blue or cold undo the whole splint and bandage. With swelling a tight splint can quickly become a tourniquet. Climbers should practise making splints before a trip; when improvising a splint in earnest, try it on the uninjured limb first.

Body splints:
the most available splint is the body itself. Splint a broken

arm to the chest and a broken leg to the opposite uninjured leg, padding between them.

Improvised splints:
imagination designs improvised splints; tape secures them.
– Arm: closed-cell foam pad; hardwood bark; newspaper, cardboard or a magazine rolled into a tube, cut to size and shaped
– Leg: tree branch or ice axe; tent pole, ski, telescopic ski pole, canoe paddle
– Ankle: down jacket, clothing
– Back: two pack-frames strapped together; a cabin door or a ladder; 2 paddles.

Walking crutch:
trim a stout sapling at a Y-junction.

Malleable splints:
Kramer wire; wire mesh ¼"; SAM splints. Bend to conform.

Inflatable splints:
place the limb in an inflatable double-skinned tube – different sizes for arms and legs. Leg splints wrap around the limb and are closed by a zip fastener or self-adhesive Velcro material. Put an arm splint over your own arm, wrist-end first. Grasp the victim's hand, as in greeting, and slide the splint from your arm onto his. Inflate a splint by mouth so you can still indent it easily with finger pressure: an over-inflated splint can cut off blood supply. Let it down every 2 hours; then re-inflate. Leave the fingers and toes open to observe their colour and temperature. Inflatable splints can be put on over clothing. If evacuating the person by air, partially deflate the splint because of pressure changes at altitude.

Plaster splints:
fibreglass casting tape is light, waterproof and durable; it

should replace plaster of Paris for wilderness rescue, even though expensive. For arm or leg, mould a back-slab onto the natural contour, encasing not more than ¾ of the circumference; the remaining gap allows any swelling of the limb to expand. Wrap the limb in a light bandage, shirt or underclothes and put the plaster over it. Hold the limb in slight traction in its normal position at rest. Don't aim at perfect position and alignment; on reaching hospital an expert can replace the cast. Never apply plaster directly to the skin; put it on over padding either of wool or the person's clothing left in place. Fold any loose ends back so the skin does not rub when the plaster hardens. To apply the plaster wear disposable surgical gloves packed together with the rolls in the medical kit.

Traction splints:
useful for lower limb fractures. For over a century the Thomas splint has been used (see page 151) by mountain rescue teams, but is bulky and heavy. For the same effect you can improvise a traction device from two pack-frames lashed together, or two ski poles.

Specific injuries

The common bony injuries in mountain accidents happen to the spine, pelvis, ribs, collar-bone, forearm, hand, lower leg, and ankle. For convenience, specific injuries are dealt with region by region.

Upper limb

For injuries around the shoulder, collar-bone (clavicle), upper arm (humerus), elbow or forearm (radius and ulna) immobilize the limb by binding it to the chest with a sling and swathe. The weight of the arm itself affords some traction

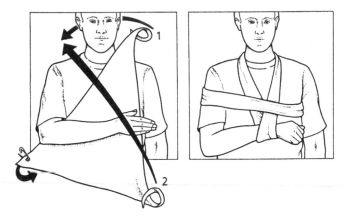

Triangular bandage, sling and swathe

to upper arm injuries. Make a forearm sling with a triangular
bandage or a collar-and-cuff. Pin the sleeve of the victim's
jacket to his opposite shoulder. Bind and splint the injured
arm to the chest with a swathe of rope or clothing, padded
for comfort.

CLAVICLE

Fractured clavicle:
the clavicle lies close under the skin so any break in its
normal contour is obvious.

  Act: a forearm sling and swathe is adequate for a day or
two; but if pain persists brace the shoulders back with a
figure-of-eight bandage tied over the jacket to prevent the
broken bone ends grating. Make two well-padded rings out
of bandage or a scarf, one for each shoulder. Windlass the
rings together to pull the shoulders back with a third tie

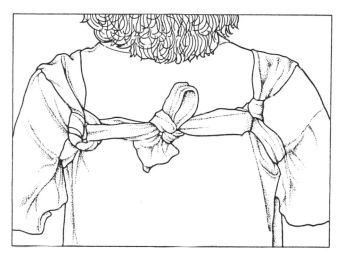

Figure-of-eight bandage

padded between it and the spine. If the hands tingle or go numb, slacken the windlass.

Acromio-clavicular joint separation:
the tip of the shoulder is very tender and hurts to move. A high step interrupts the contour.

Act: a sling makes the joint comfortable until it heals, but accurate reduction is unnecessary unless very widely separated; then a surgeon is needed.

SHOULDER

Shoulder dislocation:
a fairly common and dramatic injury whereby the head of the humerus (which forms the upper arm) slips below the

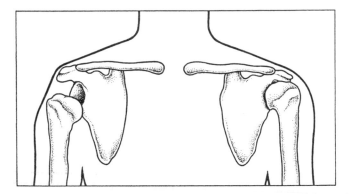

Dislocated shoulder

shallow socket (glenoid) of the shoulder blade (scapula) in which it lies. With prompt attention the shoulder of a person, disabled and in pain, can be reduced so he can still assist in his own evacuation. Every first-aider should learn how to reduce and replace a dislocated shoulder which is one of the few medical emergencies where swift, skilful intervention can alter the outcome significantly, and is satisfying to victim and rescuer alike.

A first-time dislocation, usually from a fall on an outstretched hand, must be reduced within minutes or else the powerful muscles around the shoulder lock tight in spasm because of pain. Some shoulders dislocate repeatedly, but they are usually replaced easily, often by, or under the instruction of, the victim himself.

Look: compared with the normal side the rounded contour of the dislocated shoulder becomes pointed, with the upper arm angulated away from the chest. The person supports his injured arm with his opposite hand.

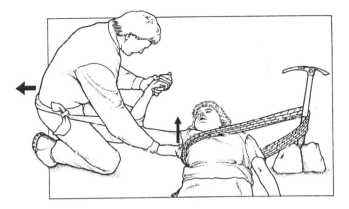

Reducing dislocated shoulder

Act: reassure him and gently massage his shoulder muscles to help them relax.

Treat: morphine (D.1.4) before attempting to reduce a dislocated shoulder.

Before doing any manoeuvre, feel for a radial pulse and test for sensation of touch. Record any abnormal findings because nerves and blood vessels may get pinched in the armpit (axilla), especially if there is an associated fracture of the neck of the humerus. A pinched circumflex nerve, a common injury, causes numbness over the outer upper arm 5cm below the tip of the shoulder.

Lie the person face down for 15 to 30 minutes with the injured arm hanging over the side of the elevated surface where he is lying. Tie a weight (e.g. a pack-sack) to the wrist of the injured side to give extra traction; this alone may reduce the shoulder. If it does not, turn the person over, have an assistant pull the arm gently to 90° from the body. Then push up firmly with both thumbs on the head of the humerus which can be felt in the armpit.

If simple measures fail try one of these 2 methods:

2-sling:
the least likely to cause further damage, but requires practice. Make slings of rolled cloth, a belt, a climbing sling, or rope. Pass one sling, well-padded, under the armpit of the dislocated shoulder; it pulls across the body (counter-traction) either towards an assistant kneeling opposite, or to a fixed point. Gently move the injured arm 90° away from the trunk (abduct), and bend (flex) the elbow to 90°.

Put the other sling first round the crook of the elbow of the injured arm, then round the rescuer's buttocks. Kneel, or squat, beside the person. With your left hand keep the victim's arm bent to 90° at the elbow, and raised to 90° from his trunk. Feel for the head of the humerus with your right hand in his armpit. Lean back into the loop sling and give a strong, steady pull on the injured arm. Rotate it slightly using his forearm, held straight out from his trunk. While pushing firmly with your right thumb on the head of the humerus, lever it gently over the lip of the joint rim (glenoid). It should slide in with a satisfying pop, and the person's face will light up with joy.

Hippocrates:
place your own socked foot high in the victim's armpit with your knee and leg straight; hold his wrist with both hands and lean backwards giving a long, steady pull on his arm while pushing with your heel. This traction will ease his pain immediately. Talk to him reassuringly to get him to relax.

After at least 5 minutes traction, gear yourself up mentally to reduce the shoulder with one strong, smooth movement; if you fail the muscles will go into spasm again and you have lost your chance. While maintaining your push-pull on his arm and using your heel as a fulcrum, lever his hand across his body. The head of the humerus should slip back into the socket with a slight clunk.

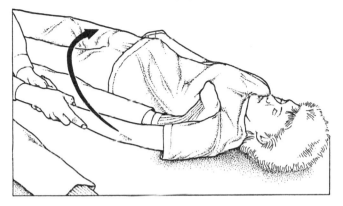

Reducing dislocated shoulder, Hippocrates method

Put the arm in a sling and bind it firmly to the chest. To exclude a fracture, have it X-rayed as soon as possible (ideally before effecting any of these manoeuvres – understandably impossible in the wilderness).

Painful shoulder:
(tendinitis, bursitis, frozen shoulder etc): many lesions around the shoulder result from bruising, injury or overuse. Movement is painful and limited.
Treat: ibuprofen (D.1.2) and rest.

Fracture of the humerus:
use a full arm sling or a collar-and-cuff wrist sling leaving the elbow unsupported to give gravity traction. Reduction is unnecessary.

ELBOW
Fractures and dislocations around the elbow are difficult to differentiate, so treat as the same. They are common in

children and especially serious because the brachial artery and nerves crossing the crook of the elbow may be damaged by the broken bone ends, or in attempts to reduce the fracture – always a difficult task.

Act: if you cannot feel the radial pulse at the wrist, always attempt reduction and hope blood flow may return. If it remains absent, splint the arm as you find it and get to a hospital fast.

Tennis Elbow (lateral epicondylitis):
the knob on the outer side of the elbow is tender on lifting a weight, shaking hands or hammering, because the origin of the extensor muscles on the back of the forearm is inflamed.

Act: place 1" tape right round the forearm 2" below the elbow knob to make a false origin for the extensor muscles. Avoid activities that hurt and be patient for 3 to 6 months.

FOREARM

Fracture of the radius and ulna:
usually occur together.

Act: splint with a slab on the back of the forearm including the elbow; swathe arm to body.

WRIST

Colles' fracture (distant end of radius and ulna):
the wrist has the shape of a dinner fork and needs reducing by a surgeon.

Act: splint the forearm with the wrist slightly cocked back, using plaster or Kramer wire moulded to the shape of the wrist.

'Sprains':
often hide an underlying fracture or a ligament tear, so always have them X-rayed.

Scaphoid fracture of the palm:
tender over the 'snuffbox' between the tendons of the extended thumb, seen when the thumb is cocked up. It may be complicated when the nearer fragment of bone loses its blood supply and dies (avascular necrosis), visible on X-ray.

Bennett's fracture (sprained thumb):
a chip at the base of the thumb metacarpal needs to be screwed into place.

Skier's thumb:
disrupted ulnar collateral ligament. The thumb is unstable and the ligament needs surgical repair.

Tendinitis:
the tendons of the wrist hurt and may creak on moving – often a result of overuse.
   Treat: ibuprofen (D.1.2), rest, ice, firm bandage.

HAND

Fractures of the small bones of the hand:
splint in a 'boxing glove' with a rolled-up sock held in the palm of the hand, and a bulky tensor bandage dressing leaving the fingers open for inspection – also a useful dressing for soft tissue injuries of the hand.

Dislocation of the finger or thumb:
obvious from the deformity. A straight pull may not be effective because tissue becomes wedged between the ends. Flex the dislocated finger joint then pull while pushing the distal finger (or toe) back on. (See diagram page 149) Splint the finger to its neighbour.

Boxing glove dressing

Tendon and nerve injuries:
are always serious; flexor tendons in the palm especially so.
Surgery is urgent.

Infected fingers:
soak in hot water. If pus shows like a boil at the base of the
nail (whitlow) or at the apex of the pulp (pulp abscess) first
freeze it with ice, then knife it to drain the pus.
    Treat: antibiotics (D.2).

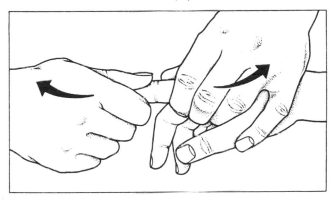

Reducing dislocated finger

Sliver or splinter under the nail:
cut a V-wedge as far back as possible and try to grasp the splinter with tweezers.

Sliced finger:
replace and hold the flap with Steri-strips. Hope it may 'take' as a graft, with full healing.

Amputation of a finger:
carry the part, immersed in saline solution in a plastic bag, to a surgeon who may be able to sew it on again, provided it arrives, chilled adequately, within 18 hours of injury.

Lower limb

HIP OR THIGH

Fracture or dislocation of the head or neck of the femur:
the difference may be difficult to tell but is important. In
neither condition will the person be able to walk and he will
have much pain in the hip. A fracture is usually caused during
a fall by landing on both feet; the hip is extended and rotated
outwards. A dislocation is caused by a force directly on the
knee bent at right angles; the hip is flexed and internally
rotated and the femur is moved towards the mid-line and cannot be straightened. Massive contraction of the buttock and
thigh muscles makes reduction extremely difficult.

Act (fracture): a Thomas splint, or one of its modern
derivatives, can windlass the foot to pull the femur straight.
Without the real thing you must rig up a traction device
from other gear at hand, like two pack-frames.

Thread the ring of the Thomas splint over the injured limb
until it abuts against the pubic bone high up in the crotch.
An assistant pulls on the victim's foot. The leg rests on
supporting slings secured with safety pins between the arms
of the splint. Tie an ankle-hitch over his boot with a bandage
and secure it to the cross end-piece of the splint. Increase
traction on the leg by windlassing the bandage, but beware
not to overtighten it. If the victim complains of pain around
the ankle-hitch, slacken the tension. With his boot on, you
cannot see the colour of his toes nor feel their temperature,
so be aware of impeding the circulation. If you cannot make
a traction device, tie two ice axes together to make a splint
from armpit to ankle. Pad the picks well. Place binders round
the whole body and bandage the bad leg to the good one
with lots of padding between the legs.

Act (dislocation): with an assistant pressing down on the
wings of the victim's pelvis, bend his knee to 90° and steady

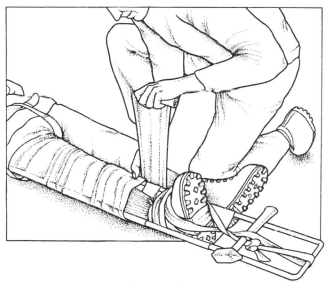

Thomas splint

his foot between your knees, Give a long, strong pull upwards and gently rotate the hip. Reducing a hip without anaesthetic is almost impossible, but far from help you must try. A Thomas splint is useless for reducing a dislocated hip.

Trochanteric bursitis:
pain develops over the protuberance of the hip, and increases on walking.
   Treat: ibuprofen (D.1.2) and rest.

Ruptured saphenous vein:
causes dramatic bruising and swelling on the inside of the thigh, which will subside unaided.

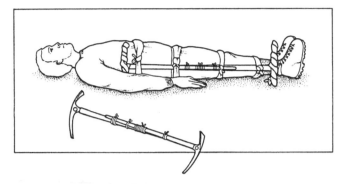

Improvised splint

KNEE

Knee fracture and dislocation:
rare and results only from violent force.

Patella fracture:
the knee is swollen and tender over the kneecap where a dent may be felt. Patella dislocation is often recurrent and the victim knows how to replace it.

Ligament or meniscus tears:
difficult to differentiate; in both the knee swells and feels unstable. Pressing over the joint line on the injured side hurts.
   Act: hold the knee straight and immobile by firm support with a crêpe bandage from thigh to ankle. The bulkier the dressing the steadier it will hold it.

Bursitis:
pain and tenderness are felt in front of the patella (house-

maids), below the patella (clergymen), or behind the hollow (climbers).

Treat: ibuprofen (D.1.2) and rest.

LOWER LEG

Fractured tibia and/or fibula:
usually both bones break, the leg is deformed and painful, and walking is impossible.

Act: splint from above the knee to below the ankle and evacuate to a surgeon.

Ruptured gastrocnemius or Achilles tendon:
the victim feels as though he has been booted in the mid-calf or above the heel. Walking is difficult and he cannot tiptoe.

Act: the calf will heal on its own; the Achilles may need surgery.

'Shin splints':
embodies a host of aches felt in the lower leg after over-use by hypochondriacal athletes. Rest is of the essence.

Thrombo-phlebitis:
the calf is tender and flexing the foot towards the knee hurts in the calf. The danger is of a clot shooting to the lungs (embolus).

Treat: analgesics (D.1), antibiotics (D.2) and rest until symptoms subside.

ANKLE

Sprains and fractures of the ankle:
occur by tripping or falling from a height. They are difficult to distinguish, especially a lateral malleolus chip-fracture (common in skiing) and may be misdiagnosed as a sprained or twisted ankle. Both are swollen and painful. Walking on

a fracture is painful. If the heels hurt suspect a fractured
calcaneum and examine the spine which may also have been
injured in the fall.

Act: pillow-splint a fracture; tape a sprain firmly making
a figure-of-eight round the ankle.

FOOT

Fractures of the small bones:
occur when something heavy drops on the foot, or after long
marching – usually the 2nd metatarsal. They are painful but
not serious, and can be strapped.

N.B. The victim of leg injury should walk if possible; dally-
ing may mean being benighted with the peril that goes with
an unplanned bivouac. To evacuate someone by stretcher is
slow, laborious and often dangerous. A broken arm should
not hinder descent, but a fractured leg will probably be too
painful to walk on and the victim must be carried. Keep
reviewing the condition of the person and of his limb as you
descend. He may need a dressing loosened, a splint adjusted,
a pee, or another dose of pain-killer.

Ingrowing toenail:
always cut toenails straight across to prevent a sliver at the
side digging in and becoming painfully infected.

Act: warm salt soaks, cut a V-wedge in the middle of the
nail.

Treat: antibiotics (D.2).

PELVIS

Fracture:
falling from a height is the commonest cause of someone
crushing the ring of pelvic bones. The pelvis is surrounded
by many muscles and hollow spaces so a severe fracture

will not be obvious; the person's only complaint may be of pain round the hips and difficulty in walking. Several pints of blood can seep away into the tissues unnoticed before he suddenly collapses from shock. He may rupture his urethra or bladder as a result of the fractured pelvis.

Act: pad between the legs with soft wool clothing and put a firm supporting binder round the upper thighs; bandage the knees and feet together to prevent the legs moving on the pelvis. Give analgesics and evacuate gently on a stretcher.

12

APPENDICITIS OR NOT

Belly

All tender bellies need a surgeon; to tell one condition from another requires skill, but your careful written observations will assist him. Until help can be reached use i/v fluids, antibiotics – and hope. Accute appendicitis is the commonest and most worrying surgical condition.

Ask: where is the pain? (pain and tenderness usually overlie the affected organs; to describe the site of the pain divide the abdomen into quarters – right and left, upper and lower, flanks to the side, loins behind). When and how did it start (exact time, sudden or gradual)? Nature of pain (dull, aching, sharp, crampy) and any change? Has pain moved? Does it radiate to another area (to the back, shoulders, genitals)? Appetite loss, indigestion, nausea, vomiting? Diarrhoea, constipation? Peeing more frequent or burning? Blood in the urine or stool?

Look: first at the victim's face. Is he well or ill, pale or flushed, hot or cold, frowning in pain or calm and relaxed? Remove clothing so you can see from chest to thigh. Scars of previous surgery? Tongue moist or dry (as in dehydration or mouth-breathing), clean or furred and smelly breath (as in appendicitis)? Does the abdomen rise with normal breathing, is it held rigid with the lower chest doing all the work? Is the belly swollen or distended; is there local swelling, especially in the hernial areas?

Feel: the pulse and temperature of the forehead using the back of the fingers. Feel gently in all quarters of the belly with the flat of a warm hand; don't dig with your fingers or he'll tense and you will learn nothing. Does the abdomen let your hand sink in or does it feel rigid, guarding the contents? Press in one spot; does it hurt in another? Watch the person's face all the while for a grimace that suggests tenderness. Only a large or solid mass will be palpable; detecting a small mass requires much experience. Gently feel the hernia areas in the groin, the scrotum and the testicles.

Listen: for normal gurgling bowel sounds with an ear placed against his belly for at least 3 minutes; tinkling sounds tell that the bowel is moving, silence suggests paralysis (ileus), possibly due to obstruction or peritonitis.

Draw a picture to record every finding.

Acute bellyache can occur in the fit, young and healthy. The most serious cause is appendicitis which, if neglected, can be deadly.

ACUTE APPENDICITIS

Appendicitis is easy to diagnose once all the classical signs are manifest, yet in its early stages it can mimic several other conditions that cause abdominal pain. The finger-like appendix lies in the right lower quarter of the abdomen. Its variable position in relation to the large bowel, and its stage of inflammation, account for the variety of signs it presents.

Symptoms and signs of appendicitis
Pain: commonly starts round the umbilicus and after about 6 hours shifts to the right lower quarter. The person feels queasy and the idea of food is revolting. Vomiting usually occurs after the onset of central pain and before it moves to the right side. Walking hurts in the right groin and the person prefers to lie still with legs drawn up.

Look: he is unwell, flushed with fever, and has a furred tongue and stinky breath. If the appendix perforates the pain eases and, owing to resulting peritonitis, he looks pale, shocked, and has a racing pulse. Ask about previous surgery; a scar suggests that the appendix has already been snatched, which should allow you to heave a sigh of relief and make an easier diagnosis.

Feel: muscles in the right lower quarter guard the tender contents of his belly, whereas the left side remains soft and empty. Press more deeply where it hurts and – once only – release the pressure suddenly, which may evoke an 'ouch!' (rebound tenderness). Bowel sounds are absent if peritonitis has spread.

Act: an inflamed appendix can burst within 24 to 36 hours spilling pus into the belly and causing peritonitis, which may kill. If no surgeon is within swift reach, stop feeding the person by mouth (because drinking will make him vomit) and give i/v fluids.

Tide the victim over till surgery using i/v normal saline or Ringer's solution run at about 3 litres over 24 hours. Suck out hourly the stomach contents by a naso-gastric tube passed through the nose (or mouth if not possible via the nose) and taped in place – drip-and-suck.

Treat: cephalosporin (D.2.1) i/v best, but i/m or oral route would do;

metronidazole (D.2.3) added to the antibiotic regime; pain-killers, generously.

If the person is not cured by this time-honoured shipboard regime, he may develop a mass with the appendix walled off by omentum (the fat-laden membrane that hangs from the bowel). An abscess forms like a time-bomb wrapped in a protective coat for later dismantling by a surgeon. The worst scenario is when the appendix bursts spilling pus into the peritoneum (peritonitis); in this case double all the antibiotic dosages.

The following conditions, arranged roughly in order of

frequency, mimic appendicitis and must be excluded when faced with acute low bellyache. In every case consult a surgeon as soon as possible because accurate diagnosis is very difficult in the wilderness.

CONSTIPATION

Inadequate drinking, lack of fresh fruit, eating dehydrated food, and medication containing morphine or codeine cause constipation. Prove with a laxative suppository or an enema; like clearing a log jam, it's best approached from below. An impacted, rock-hard stool may be the result of dehydration and constipation owing to being stormbound in a tent and not drinking enough melted snow. If the stool is impacted, push a greased finger high in the rectum, break the hard stool and withdraw it in pieces. A soapy-water enema will flush out the residue.

GASTRO-ENTERITIS

Crampy pain, profuse and watery diarrhoea, and nausea and vomiting are usual. The story may be of eating strange food (e.g. Tibetan tea) or of other members of the party being similarly stricken. Giardiasis occurs where beavers live in the water, and in the Himalaya and other wild regions. The belly rumbles and churns, diarrhoea comes and goes (sometimes urgently), along with rank burps and sulphurous farts.

Act: avoid eating, drink plenty; diarrhoea will probably cease in 24 to 48 hours, but if not:

Treat: metronidazole (D.2.3) against the Giardia, and loperamide (D.9.3.).

URINARY TRACT INFECTION

The sufferer, commonly female, pees frequently (every 15 to 30 minutes), which feels like passing powdered glass. Murky, smelly urine may be tinged with blood. Pain and tenderness are felt in the flank (kidney infection, pyelitis), or above the pubis (bladder infection, cystitis), which mimic an inflamed appendix in contact with the ureter or bladder. Despite a high fever she shakes with chills.

Act: fluids in plenty with baking soda added to make the urine alkaline and less clement to acid-loving E. coli.

Treat: co-trimoxazole (D.2.2).

STONE IN THE URETER

A dull ache is felt in the loin so long as a stone remains in the kidney. When a small stone passes down the ureter (connecting kidneys and bladder) it causes agonizing colic ('the worst pain I've ever felt'). Small stones, like small dogs, make most noise. The victim rolls around with steady pain, starting in the loin and moving towards the groin, and often into the genitals. Pain comes in waves, builds to a crescendo with vomiting, and then dies down leaving a dull ache. Frequent urine may be blood-stained.

Act: drink plenty to flush out the stone, use strong pain-killers, and meditate whilst waiting for its passing.

ACUTE GALL-BLADDER

Fatty foods cause indigestion; and constant severe pain, felt high under the right ribs, travels through to the back, to the bottom of the lower right shoulder blade, or to the right shoulder tip. A low-slung gall-bladder may cause pain down to the right lower quarter like appendicitis. However, it is more likely to be confused with a peptic ulcer or an inflamed oesophagus. Yellow jaundice suggests a stone obstructing the flow of bile, and causing pale stools and dark urine.

Act: rest and give limited fluids. Most attacks subside without surgery.

Treat: codeine (D.1.3), (not morphine, which constricts the bile duct exit);

　　　　　antibiotics (D.2).

WOMEN'S PROBLEMS

Pain from the right ovary or right fallopian tube can mimic
appendicitis.

Ovary pain:
ask any woman complaining of low bellyache the date of
her last period, and whether she could be pregnant. Normal
pre-menstrual pains are sometimes quite disabling. If the
date is exactly half-way between her periods she may be
ovulating normally with slight bleeding from the ovarian
follicle into the peritoneum (mittelschmertz) causing acute
pain and tenderness lingering for a few hours.

Salpingitis:
infection of the fallopian tubes is usually accompanied by
smelly vaginal discharge. Fever is high and pain is felt on
both sides low down, but it may be over the appendix only,
which confuses the diagnosis.

If she is pregnant beware of:

Abortion (miscarriage):
the story is of a missed period, heavy vaginal bleeding, and
generalized cramps with passing of clots.
   Treat: [ergometrine] 0.25 mg i/m.

Ectopic pregnancy:
pregnancy develops on rare occasions outside the womb in
one or other fallopian tube, which can suddenly burst, causing profuse bleeding into the belly.
   Act: only surgery avails; i/v fluids may help meanwhile.

INTESTINAL OBSTRUCTION

Any part of the bowel, large or small, may become obstructed by a multitude of causes, mostly too academic to discuss
here. But look for a scar from previous surgery suggesting

adhesions, or a hernia that may have twisted. The bowel may distend, strangulate, die and burst, leading to fatal peritonitis. Any obstruction on the right side of the belly may ape appendicitis. An obstructed person looks sick and has pain, vomiting, distension and absolute constipation.

Treat: pain-killers (D.1), and antibiotics, cephalosporin (D.2.1) and metronidazole (D.2.3). Drip-and-suck.

PEPTIC ULCER

Ulcers in the stomach or duodenum can exist for years without causing more than vague indigestion and discomfort in the pit of the stomach coming on 1 to 2 hours after eating. Avoid fried foods, coffee, alcohol and cigarettes but drink milk. An ulcer may bleed or perforate suddenly and catastrophically.

Treat: aluminium hydroxide (D.9.1), cimetidine (D.9.2).

Bleeding ulcer:
the victim feels faint and sweaty, vomits bright-red or coffee-ground blood (haematemesis) and becomes shocked. Diarrhoea may follow some hours later with dark, tarry stools (melaena).

Act: drip-and-suck until it is possible to replace blood with blood;

Treat: cimetidine (D.9.2).

Perforation:
sudden pain in the upper abdomen can mimic a heart attack or a perforated appendix. 3 to 4 litres of noxious, toxic stomach contents spill spreading bacteria throughout the belly and causing peritonitis. The pain worsens steadily with vomiting and a rising pulse. Deceptively, he may begin to improve before collapsing with a tender rigid abdomen. Breathing is shallow, and he looks, and is, deathly.

Treat: morphine (D.1.4), cephalosporin (D.2.1), metronidazole (D.2.3); drip-and-suck; evacuate urgently.

HERNIA

Gut or omentum may protrude through the muscular abdominal wall, usually in the groin, following the strain of carrying heavy loads. The resulting hernia may slide back on lying down, with the help of firm manual pressure. But gut may be nipped off and become strangulated, gangrenous and perforated. The tense, tender swelling in the groin cannot be pushed back; the victim vomits copiously, has griping pains, a distended belly and is shocked.

In a tent north of Dhaulagiri in the Himalayas I once came across a Tibetan lama who looked just like this. After giving him a dose of morphine and a mug of 'rakshi' spirits, I tried to squeeze the hernia back – to no avail. With two Sherpas holding him down, another monk chanting mantras, some local anaesthetic, and a small suture kit I operated on him, untwisted the bowel and sewed him up. Ten minutes later a thunderous fart announced our luck and his life. Such surgery is neither recommended nor approved by the Royal Colleges.

TESTICLE

Sudden pain without a story of injury is likely to be due either to acute inflammation or to torsion of the testicle, which must be untwisted urgently.

Act: support the scrotum in a tight pair of underpants well-padded with cotton wool. Cautiously and gently attempt to unwind the torsion, and don't make him laugh.

Treat: cephalosporin (D.2.1).

PILES (HAEMORRHOIDS)

Piles pop out when the pressure within the abdomen rises from straining at stool or carrying heavy loads with over-breathing (especially at high altitudes). Always uncomfortable and inconvenient when prolapsed, piles feel like grapes,

or varicose veins, at the anal margin; they can be very painful. Bright blood appears on the toilet paper after passing
stool, and there is slimy, itchy discharge.

Act: have troublesome piles shrunk by a surgeon's needle
(surprisingly painless) before setting out on a trip. If already
embarked, take bran to soften the stool, and drink enough
fluid to prevent constipation (avoid morphine or codeine).
Keep scrupulously clean because soiling with faeces causes
maddening itch. Push prolapsed piles back inside the anus
quickly to avoid them swelling and staying out. Dropping
your trousers at 7,000m (20,000ft) in a blizzard is bad
enough, but having prolapsed piles as well is the ultimate
misery.

Treat: bismuth subgallate (D.9.5) haemorrhoidal cream or
suppository.

13

ABDOMINAL INJURY

The abdomen houses 9m (28ft) of gut and several major organs – liver, spleen, kidneys, bladder. The entire cavity and the organs themselves are enveloped in a thin membrane of peritoneum which allows gut to move around without friction. Peritoneum senses pain when stretched or irritated by noxious fluids or blood.

Serious injury to the abdomen, whether blunt (closed) or sharp (penetrating), may cause internal bleeding or leakage of gut contents, faeces, pus or urine; any or all of these cause peritonitis. Be alert, even after a minor blow, for possible internal mischief not immediately manifest. Surgery is the treatment for most abdominal injuries.

Closed abdominal injury

Ask about the nature of the object causing the injury, and how the accident happened (e.g. falling across a rock, or onto an ice axe).

SIGNS AND SYMPTOMS OF CLOSED ABDOMINAL INJURY OR MISCHIEF

Pain:
varies greatly; if severe the victim lies quite still. Pain starts around the umbilicus but spreads and settles in the region of

the injured organ. Noxious fluids in contact with the under surface of the diaphragm irritate the phrenic nerve and refer pain to one or both shoulder tips.

Tenderness:
is general with guarding over the injured organs. If peritonitis spreads, the abdominal muscles feel rigid, like pressing on a board. Further pressure causes pain, especially on removing the examining hand suddenly (rebound tenderness).

Shock:
is always present after internal bleeding. A person in shock is pale, sweaty and cold with a rapid, feeble pulse: so if there is no external bleeding look to the abdomen for the cause. Shock is uncommon in head injury.

Vomiting:
preceded by nausea is a constant sign of abdominal mischief, especially peritonitis. Bleeding from the stomach is rare in abdominal trauma, so if bright-red fresh blood appears in the vomit look for an injured nose, mouth or tongue.

Blood in the urine:
damage to the kidneys or bladder is likely; blood at the end of the penis suggests injury to the urethra.

Breathing:
is quiet, the lower chest moves but the abdomen is still.

Act: Reassure the person, who may be flippant about an injury you suspect is not trivial. Warn him of possible serious consequences and descend as soon as possible.

Rest completely and allow only sips of water by mouth as he may vomit (but dry = restless). Don't worry about fluid in his stomach; this is the hospital anaesthetist's problem, not yours, and he has means to deal with it.

Record all observations on paper every half hour, especially the pulse rate and any change in his condition.

Treat: morphine (D.1.4) relieves pain and allays anxiety, but it causes vomiting; so give promethazine (D.3.1) as well. Do not withhold analgesics for fear of masking pain from the doctor who will try to diagnose him later; he can reverse the effects of morphine with naloxone (D.1.5). Always write the drug name, the dose, and the time given on a label and attach it to the patient for the information of the receiving doctor.

Infection:
the stage is set because spilt intestinal contents teem with bacteria, and blood is an ideal medium for growing bugs. Give large doses of broad spectrum antibiotics (D.2).

SPECIFIC CLOSED INJURIES

Spleen:
quite trivial force can rupture the spleen. Fractured left lower ribs may impale the underlying spleen. So always suspect abdominal organ rupture after a chest injury, especially on the left. Progressive severe bleeding with shock is usual after rupture, but silent symptomless bleeding may continue from several hours to 3 weeks beneath the enfolding capsule, which will stretch and suddenly burst, spilling blood into the peritoneum. The person becomes deeply shocked. Evacuate anyone suffering an abdominal injury in the wilderness, however mild, because of the danger of secondary haemorrhage.

Liver:
caused by a crushing blow to the upper abdomen or fracture of the lower right ribs. Minor tears often stop bleeding, but in massive injury it continues unabated. Occasionally bleeding

continues under the capsule (similar to the spleen) with sudden catastrophic rupture after a delay of some hours.

Kidney:
caused by a direct blow in the loin or flank, possibly with a fracture of the 12th rib. Pain is local when bleeding is contained within the capsule of the kidney, and blood is usually seen in the urine (haematuria). All may resolve with rest alone.

Urethra:
a tear occurs when a fractured segment of pelvis (to which the urethra is tethered) is pulled apart, or after falling astride a solid object like a tree or onto a rock. The victim, most commonly a man, has severe pain in the crotch, which is badly bruised between the scrotum and the anus. Look for fresh blood at the end of the penis. He cannot pee so the bladder becomes distended and can be felt above the pubic bone after some hours, and it is very uncomfortable. Urine and blood, instead of passing down the damaged urethra, may spread up into the muscle planes of the lower abdomen or of the perineum which readily become infected.

Treat: broad spectrum antibiotic (D.2) immediately.

No harm can come from 24 hours of inactivity, but attempting to pass a catheter may damage the few remaining strands by which the urethra can recanalize itself. Leave catheters to a waterworks specialist because meddling now may make the urethra irreparable later.

Far from help, if his bladder swells after waiting 24 hours, plunge a wide bore sterile needle through the cleansed skin of the abdominal wall in the mid-line 2cm (1") above the pubic bone at least 5cm (2") deep (bladder is close against abdominal wall with nothing else intervening at this point), and let urine spurt out. Repeated stabs, perhaps every 8 hours or whenever the bladder appears full, are less likely to cause infection than leaving an indwelling needle or canula.

Bladder:
rupture is rare.

Act: suprapubic drainage (as above).

Treat: antibiotics (D.2) will tide him over until he can reach a surgeon.

Open abdominal injury

Guts or fatty omentum may protrude in the rare event of an open wound from a knife, ice axe or gun-shot – a horrendous sight. Do no try to push them back inside, but cover the wound with a clean, preferably sterile, damp dressing. If the instrument that caused the injury is still in the wound, and if you can reach help quickly, leave it there because it may be plugging the hole like the Dutch boy's finger in the dyke. However, if it is in a major blood vessel it may wriggle free during transport, which would be fatal. You may then have to take a chance and remove it.

A small puncture wound of the skin should cause you as much anxiety as an obvious gash. You can only guess whether the instrument has nicked the skin and penetrated muscle, or whether it has pierced an internal organ. A long sharp object, like a knife, which punctures the skin can be withdrawn leaving barely a mark, but punctured bowel may seal over temporarily and leak noxious fluid later – with a fatal outcome. Most surgeons assume that a puncture wound has penetrated the abdominal cavity until proved otherwise, and operate forthwith.

14

SUNDRY MEDICAL ILLS

Heart and chest

The symptoms and signs of heart and chest illness frequently
overlap. The person may complain of chest pain, irregular
heartbeat, cough, or difficulty and shortness of breathing.
To reach a diagnosis, weigh the history and examination
findings. Only conditions reasonably likely to be encountered in the outdoors are described here.

Ask the person for any past history of heart or chest disease. Is he now taking any medications? Look for a Medic-
Alert bracelet or medallion. Allergies? Smoker? Overweight?

Chest pain:
ask the nature of the pain and its manner of onset (sudden
or gradual).

Sharp – described as stabbing or knife-like. Pain that is
worsened on inspiration, usually on one side only and often
referred to the shoulder or abdomen probably arises from
the lung surface (pleurisy). Pain localized precisely to one
tender rib may be due to fracture. Chest wall pain is accentu-
ated by movement.

Dull – also described as gripping, vice-like, crushing, constricting. Angina typically is pain, pressure or tightness in
the centre or left side of the chest, or deep behind the sternum, possibly referred to the shoulder or arms or up into
the neck or jaw. It comes on with exertion and is relieved

by rest, usually in someone with known heart disease. Heart attack (myocardial infarction) may be associated with shortness of breath and sweaty, nauseating shock.

Pulse:
rapid and regular – can occur in healthy people, causing an uncomfortable feeling like butterflies behind the sternum. It may be due to paroxysmal atrial tachycardia (PAT) which engenders anxiety but usually needs no treatment; rarely it may be serious and cause shock. Simple tachycardia (rapid pulse) may be caused by fever or oxygen lack (hypoxia) especially at altitude.
Rapid and irregular – suggests heart disease; if it accompanies chest pain think of myocardial infarction.
Slow (bradycardia) – many athletes run a pulse of less than 50 beats/minute. It can also occur in heart block from myocardial infarction.

Cough:
sudden, violent coughing and choking may be due to an inhaled foreign body. A dry cough occurs in early bronchitis; later, yellow or green sputum appears. Bright-red or rusty blood-flecked sputum suggests pneumonia, which is often accompanied by fever and rigors. Pulmonary oedema causes a dry cough with no sputum, less commonly a moist cough with pink, frothy sputum. The dry air at altitude causes irritating cough, which may crack a rib.

Shortness of breath (dyspnoea):
upper airway obstruction may be accompanied by noisy, croupy, whooping stridor, worse during inspiration
– air in the pleural cavity arises from collapse of lung (pneumothorax – spontaneous or traumatic); fluid comes from an effusion possibly after pneumonia
– stiffness of the lung owing to congestion or consolidation (pneumonia) or oedema due to heart failure caused by

myocardial infarction, is often accompanied by dyspnoea on lying down and swelling of the ankles.

Wheeze:
noisy wheezing and dyspnoea, especially during expiration and sometimes with cyanosis, suggests asthma or bronchitis. An asthma attack may be provoked in a susceptible person by contact with an allergen (e.g. pollen, dust, feathers, animal fur or certain foods). Other causes are chest infection (bronchitis or pneumonia) or emotional upset.

Sputum:
thick yellow or green spit suggests chest infection.
   Treat: antibiotic (D.2)

Heart

Look for swelling of the ankles that pits on finger pressure and shows the imprint of sock elastic, indicating heart failure. Look for the colour and nutrition of the skin of the extremities.

Raised jugular venous pressure indicates right heart failure.

Cyanosis:
a bluish colour of the skin and lips will appear in full daylight but can be missed in the poor lighting of a coloured tent. Weather-beaten, sun-tanned skin may disguise cyanosis, which occurs in two forms:
   Peripheral: seen best in the beds of the finger-nails and the lips, is due to sluggish flow of cold blood. Their normal pink colour returns on warming; the tongue remains pink. Peripheral cyanosis occurs in shock when the blood pressure falls due to circulatory failure.

Central: tongue, lips and mucous membranes inside the mouth are blue and do not turn pink on rewarming.

Central cyanosis indicates serious disturbance of heart and lung function because of either inadequate ventilation, uneven distribution of blood, decreased diffusion of oxygen or abnormal shunting of blood within the chambers of the heart. It is common at high altitude because of diminished oxygen (hypoxia) and excessive red blood cell production (polycythaemia). To judge cyanosis at altitude, compare a healthy person with the sick one. Central cyanosis disappears on breathing 100% oxygen for 10 minutes.

Feel the pulse and gauge the blood pressure (or measure it with a sphygmomanometer). Light finger-touch can tell whether the pulse is full and bounding, or weak and thready.

The apex beat, if displaced to the left, indicates an enlarged heart. Feel the peripheral pulses; femoral, posterior tibial and dorsalis pedis, to assess the peripheral circulation. Listen to the heart sounds, preferably with a stethoscope, if not, with an ear placed against the person's chest. Only a trained ear can interpret abnormal heart sounds and rhythms.

HEART ATTACK (myocardial infarction)
Severe chest pain, shock, and rapid breathing occur. Coma is unusual.
Treat: morphine (D.1.4) for pain relief. Rest and oxygen help cyanosis. If the heart stops, start rescue breathing and chest compression. Seek urgent medical help.

Chest

Look at the chest, bared from chin to belly button. Note the rate, depth and rhythm of chest movements – don't peer closely, but stand 2m back. One side of the chest may move less well than the other in pneumonia or collapsed lung (pneumothorax). The accessory muscles strain when breathing is laboured – flared nostrils, gasping mouth, taut neck muscles and indrawn intercostal muscles between the ribs.

Feel by placing hands lightly against the sides of his chest with fingers pointing towards the armpits. Unequal movement can be felt more easily on deep breathing. Percussion of the chest (thumping with one finger against a finger of the other hand placed against the chest) is hard to interpret even for a trained physician.

Listen to both sides of the chest, front and back, from top to bottom, from one side to the other, with the victim breathing gently through his mouth. You should hear equal air entry on both sides and clear, unrestricted breath sounds. Wheeze appears on expiration. Fluid in the air passages sounds like rough crumpling of paper, or fine crackling of rubbing hair between fingers in front of the ear (crepitations). At high altitude think of pulmonary oedema.

Asthma, bronchitis, and pneumonia may be difficult to distinguish.

ASTHMA

Spasm of the bronchi causes wheezing especially on expiration, a tight chest and dry cough. Feel the pulse racing and listen for crackles and expiratory wheeze. Asthma is associated with hay fever and eczema: it may be precipitated by acute infection, aspirin, specific allergens (pollens, dust), exertion, excitement and cold air.

Treat: salbutamol (D.8.1) puffer; if it does not settle, a course of prednisone (D.4.1). In a severe asthmatic attack, adrenaline (D.7.2).

Status asthmaticus:
is an attack of asthma lasting more than 24 hours. The symptoms are like asthma together with shortness of breath and cyanosis. The victim becomes drowsy and can rapidly slide into shock and die.

Treat: salbutamol (D.8.1), prednisone (D.4.1).

HYPERVENTILATION (benign)
Very anxious people may overbreathe, thereby washing carbon dioxide (their main stimulus for breathing) out of the blood. They feel dizzy or light-headed, short of breath, with sharp chest pain; hands and feet may be blue, cold, numb or tingling. Fear of a heart attack or stroke compounds the anxiety, increasing the overbreathing to the point of fainting – which may be curative by allowing normal breathing to recover.

If you are sure the hyperventilation and fainting are not due to a more serious problem, try reassurance and encourage slow regular breathing. Only use breathing into a brown paper bag in a young person with healthy heart and lungs.

BRONCHITIS
Infection of the upper respiratory tract, the common cold, laryngitis or pharyngitis, are all commonly caused by viruses; a superimposed secondary bacterial infection may develop with wheeze, fever and cough with yellow or green spit, and chest crackles.

PNEUMONIA
Pneumonia may be bacterial or viral; it causes cough with rusty or bloody sputum, fever and rigors. Breathing is rapid and painful owing to pleurisy.

Act (similar for bronchitis and pneumonia): to liquefy

secretions inhale steam from a kettle or billycan of boiling water, with a teaspoonful of tincture of benzoin or a pinch of menthol crystals added. Concentrate the steam by placing a towel over the head like a tent, but beware of scalding. Sip a cup of boiling water, adding one tablespoon each of baking soda and salt. Thump the chest with the person lying on alternating sides, tipped head down.

Treat: salbutamol (D.8.1), a bronchial relaxant, in a mild attack of bronchospasm

codeine (D.1.3) at night dampens cough to allow sleep but do not use it by day

cephalosporin (D.2.1) or co-trimoxazole (D.2.2) antibiotic for at least 1 week if sputum is yellow or green, or if there is fever

morphine (D.1.4) for severe pleuritic pain to allow full breathing (but be prepared to reverse with naloxone (D.1.5))

dexamethasone (D.4.2) i/v, or a short course of steroids, prednisone (D.4.1) by mouth, for people previously on steroids; it may help in asthma

oxygen: relieves breathlessness and cyanosis

ALLERGY

The body responds to some foreign substances (antigens) by forming protein antibodies in the blood. An excessive stimulus may cause an allergic (hypersensitivity) reaction owing to release of histamine. For example, some people are mildly sensitive to penicillin and break out in a rash; severe reactions may cause life-threatening anaphylactic shock. Common allergies result from contact with pollens and moulds, house dust and house mites, animal dander and hair, and certain foods like shellfish and chocolate. The symptoms, uncomfortable but not dangerous, are of asthma, hay fever (with running nose and eyes), or hives on the skin with itchy raised weals.

Treat: antihistamine (D.3) allays itching and speeds the disappearance of symptoms.

ANAPHYLAXIS

Immediate, severe, shock-like and often fatal reactions follow contact with an antigen – a bee or wasp sting, a drug (especially penicillin and aspirin), injection of immune serum (tetanus antiserum and snake antivenin) or, rarely, of vaccines. The symptoms are apprehension and shock, choking, wheezy asthma with cough and cyanosis. Blotchy skin weals develop all over the body; untreated, the victim may lose consciousness, convulse and die within 5 to 10 minutes.

People with known sensitivity to bee or wasp stings should carry a first-aid kit with a preloaded syringe of adrenaline (Epi Pen).

Treat: adrenaline 0.3–1.0ml of 1:1000, i/m or s/c repeated in the first 5 to 10 minutes. Keep open the victim's airway and place him in the draining position. Put up i/v fluids. [Hydrocortisone] 100–250mg i/v in the first 30 minutes followed by a course of prednisone orally.

GALL-BLADDER DISEASE

Mild gall-bladder inflammation (cholecystitis) causes indigestion and constant pain under the right rib margin, which may radiate to the right shoulder tip and/or through to the back under the right shoulder blade. Jaundice, seen as yellow whites of the eyes and a tinge to the skin, may be present with pale, putty-coloured stools and mahogany-dark urine. Food is nauseating.

A severe gall-bladder attack owing to a gall-stone lodged in the duct causes excruciating colic; the victim is very sick and needs urgent surgical help.

Treat: cephalosporin (D.2.1) may resolve cholecystitis.

JAUNDICE

Infectious hepatitis A and B is the most likely cause of jaundice in travellers. The person feels rotten for about a week before the whites of the eyes turn yellow and the skin begins to itch, eventually going yellow (but he may feel better once jaundice appears). Pain is usually absent. Full recovery may take months and be prolonged if rest, which is the only treatment, is curtailed.

Prevention is by either vaccine or immune serum (gamma) globulin.

Several infectious diseases, especially those caused by viruses, have a similar prodrome of malaise before the illness becomes manifest, e.g., influenza and glandular fever (mononucleosis).

Skin problems

ECZEMA (dermatitis): associated with allergies and contact with certain drugs, nickel and cosmetics.

Treat: betamethasone (D.11.1) ointment.

IMPETIGO: a superficial infection of the skin, usually by a staphylococcus. A vesicle becomes a pustule that forms characteristic yellow crusty scabs, commonly on the face.

Treat: cephalosporin (D.2.1) by mouth.

TINEA: a fungal infection causing athlete's foot, or dhobie itch of the crotch, manifests as a red, silver-scaly rash and is very irritating.

Treat: clotrimazole (D.11.2) antifungal cream.

SCABIES: the mite thrives in bedding and unclean clothing. It burrows forming a pinhead vesicle, which is maddeningly irritating and invites scratching especially when warm in bed.

Treat: [malathion lotion] 0.5% applied from neck to toes once and left for 24 hours.

LICE and NITS: look for eggs laid on hair shafts.
Treat: [malathion lotion] 0.5% as directed.

Sexually transmitted disease (STD)

Some nasty strains of penicillin-resistant gonococci (causing gonorrhoea), treponema (causing syphilis), and herpes virus exist abroad. But these pall in importance compared with HIV infection and its resultant AIDS (auto-immune deficiency syndrome). In some African countries half the males and females are infected, and the East is rapidly catching up. If sexually desperate, either use a hand or a condom. AIDS can also be acquired from unsterile injections (particularly in i/v drug users) and blood transfusions.

Act: don't: it's safer. But if caught with your pants down, and if a pussy urethral discharge and painful peeing come on following an impromptu sexual contact, get to a VD specialist clinic quick.

Treat: [amoxycillin] 500mg every 8 hours for 10 days, or cephalosporin (D.2.1).

Psychological upset

Psychological problems are usually alleviated by the peace of the hills, which many of us choose as our escape from worldly cares. However when anxiety supervenes we must distinguish panic from psychosis.

PANIC

Under arduous conditions, or during a difficult wilderness journey, a person may lose his nerve and become frightened, agitated and acutely anxious. Although rational, he is paralysed with fear and becomes ineffective.

Act: talk the person down with calm reassurance; anger will only provoke him. If still out of control when back at camp.

Treat: lorazepam (D.5.1). Wait until next morning to see if he returns to normal after a good sleep; if he does, the condition is panic and not psychosis, which would take much longer to settle. The person will probably be deeply ashamed of the episode, so encourage him to talk and get it off his chest. Such emotions might be the lot of any of us on another occasion, so be genuinely empathetic.

PSYCHOSIS (madness)

Madness, as distinct from panic, does not usually start out of the blue without some previous warning of mental imbalance. In selecting companions trust your intuition to be wary of someone with a record of strange behaviour. The person may lose touch with reality and have bizarre hallucinations. He feels that other people are ganging up on him, and may appear so convincing that you begin to wonder who is crazy, you or he. He tends to over-react to normal situations and may be violent and excited, or passive and withdrawn. Once the acute phase of a psychotic episode has passed, a more drawn-out depression sets in, when the person is most likely to attempt suicide.

Treat: lorazepam (D.5.1) will sedate the person; if he becomes violent try to prevent him from injuring himself and others. Forcible restraint may only worsen the situation, making him more excited, but it may be needed in the last resort.

15

POISONS AND DRUG ABUSE

INHALED GAS

Carbon monoxide is a by-product of most camping stoves. Toxic gas can accumulate in an unventilated tent or snow cave. If camping in vans in cold weather it is dangerous to leave the engine running to heat the cab because of leaking exhaust fumes. Carbon monoxide is odourless so a small amount in a tightly-closed space gives little warning other than a headache, laboured breathing, ringing in the ears, dizziness and blurred vision. Near death, the victim may be unconscious and with bright-pink skin.

Act: remove him to fresh air immediately, keep an open airway and give assisted breathing, with oxygen if possible. A vicious headache will develop during recovery.

SWALLOWED POISONS

Most drugs swallowed accidentally or intentionally must be got rid of before being absorbed into the blood. Give an emetic made of milk followed by a strong salty drink, and stick a finger down the throat. A stomach wash-out will evacuate poison, provided it is done within 4 hours of swallowing. Leave corrosives, acids and industrial poisons in the stomach because, if vomited, they will burn the oesophagus. Dilute them with large volumes of water and/or milk or white of egg.

Act: stomach wash-out only if the person is conscious, can protect his own airway, and mechanical suction is at hand. Lie

him on the left side and pass a well-lubricated tube, at least
1cm diameter, down the throat into the stomach. Attach a funnel, hold it high and pour in a litre of water. Lower the funnel
below the level of the stomach and let the fluid run out. Repeat
until the washings are clear – at least 6 times.

Drug abuse

Alcohol is the most common drug used, and abused; it
loosens social restraints and gives a false sense of bravado,
but depresses the nervous system and impairs all reactions.
Alcohol compounds the effect of some other drugs and
dangerously increases heat loss.

Strange behaviour, especially after a prolonged boring spell
in camp, may suggest a person is stoned on other drugs. Prevent him harming himself, maintain an open airway, talk him
down in a quiet place and give calm reassurance. Do not leave
him unattended until he has emerged from his trip.

COMMONLY ABUSED DRUGS

Hallucinogens – LSD (acid), PCP (angel dust), psilocybin
(magic mushrooms): cause hallucinations, agitation and
excitement. Pupils dilate (except with PCP).

Treat: lorazepam (D.5.1).

Narcotics – heroin, morphine, codeine, meperidine and
methadone cause seizures, coma and depressed breathing;
pupils are pin-point.

Treat: naloxone (D.1.5) reverses narcotics and restores
breathing. Vomiting may need suction. Control seizures
with lorazepam (D.5.1), preferably given i/v. Watch the
person closely for 24 hours because his breathing may quit,
needing resuscitation and more naloxone.

*   *   *

Cannabis group – marihuana, hashish: eyes are bloodshot, pupils unchanged and the pulse races.

Nervous system depressants 'downers' – barbiturates, diazepam (Valium), chlordiazepoxide (Librium), glutethamide (Doriden), methalqualone (Quaaludes): the depressant effect is enhanced by alcohol. Severe withdrawal symptoms occur.

Nervous system stimulants 'uppers' – amphetamines (speed), cocaine, 'crack' cocaine, anti-obesity drugs: pupils dilate but react to light, breathing is shallow, and pulse races. Seizures can occur.

Treat: lorazepam (D.5.1)

Anti-cholinergics – atropine (belladonna), tricyclic antidepressants, Jimson weed, henbane, mandrake: pupils are dilated and fixed, pulse races, skin is dry.

Other poisons

FUNGI

Avoid all wild mushrooms unless you are absolutely certain they are safe. Violent vomiting, diarrhoea and abdominal cramps come on 8 hours after eating the fungi.

Act: give repeated cups of hot tea, an emetic of salty water and Epsom salts; empty the bowel by a soap and water enema.

BOTULISM

Home-canned, or bottled food may harbour Clostridium botulinum; seal meat is notorious. Double vision, paralysis of various muscles and abdominal discomfort come on after 6 to 24 hours, often in several participants of the same meal.

Act: seek expert help urgently for [botulinus antitoxin] 50,000U i/m stat.

16

EYES

The eyeball holds terror for many people, and few can even bring themselves to inspect it closely; but only careful observation, preferably with magnification, will allow intelligent treatment.

Ask the victim to read newsprint of various sizes from normal reading distance, with each eye separately, and using glasses if usually worn. Recording the vision now will help in following progress. Was each eye normal before the present problem arose? Is the eye painful? Scratches of the window of the eye (cornea) commonly feel like a foreign body; infection of the conjunctiva (the thin, loose, transparent membrane over the white sclera) feels like sand in the eyes. Are there blurred patches in the vision, persistent flashes of light, or strange visual sensations? – all are abnormal.

Look at the eye with a flashlight and a magnifying glass, a loupe or an inverted camera lens. To make your task easier, put a drop of local anaesthetic (D.12.4) in the gutter of the lid (fornix) to ease the pain so he will relax his tightly screwed-up eyes; it acts instantaneously.

Lids:
pull down the lower lid to search for a foreign body in the fornix and then evert the upper lid where uninvited matter often lodges. When anaesthetized, sweep a match-stick, tipped with cotton wool, along both upper and lower for-

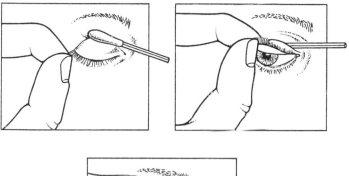

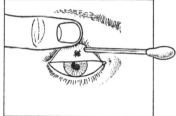

Everting eyelid

nices. If nothing appears, leave some eye ointment in the lower fornix and a foreign body may eventually float out.

Lashes:
inturned lashes scratch the cornea like barbs and are the source of much discomfort. Pluck them out with tweezers.

Conjunctiva:
red, swollen conjunctiva denotes inflammation or infection, which causes aversion to bright light, tearing, and a yellow discharge.

Cornea:
is normally clear and shiny. If fluorescein dye from a damp-
ened impregnated paper strip is touched against the inner
aspect of the lower lid, any breach in the corneal surface
caused by abrasions, ulcers or foreign bodies shows up as
a bright-green stain.

Pupil:
is normally circular and constricts to light; an eccentric pupil
suggests problems in the anterior chamber of the eye, or
penetrating trauma.

Act: dark glasses or a pirate's patch keep out light, which
is painful. A firm bandage over several eye pads puts pressure on the lids to stop blinking (which irritates the cornea).
An eye pad held on with sticky tape alone does not press
firmly enough to keep the lids closed: it becomes loose,
damp and uncomfortable.

Treat: Tea contains tannic acid which is astringent, soothing, cheap, available and there is no limit to its use. For an
uncomfortable, scratchy, painful eye squeeze cold tea from
a moist tea bag (floor sweepings quality is strongest) into
the lower fornix.

Local anaesthetic (D.12.4) 'freezes' the eye allowing
foreign bodies to be removed. Cover the eye afterwards until
sensation returns. Local anaesthetic delays healing so must
not be used over a long period to relieve pain, but allowing
a snowblind person to return to a lower camp could be
life-saving.

Mydriatic – homatropine 2% (D.12.3) twice daily
dilates the pupil and relieves painful spasm that follows
abrasion or injury of the cornea; it blurs vision making the
eye sensitive to light, so use dark glasses or a patch. Homatropine is short-acting lasting for 24 hours after the last drop,
unlike atropine which dilates the pupil for a couple of weeks.
The remote chance of inducing glaucoma should not dis-

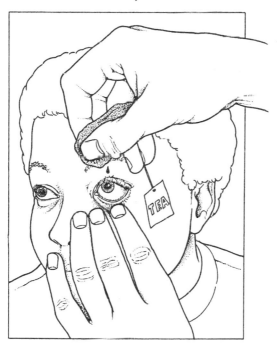

Eye drops

courage the use of a short-acting mydriatic; besides relieving pain it also offers a better view of the back of the eye for someone with the skill to use an ophthalmoscope. However, do not use it with head injury because the pupil size helps the diagnosis of cerebral compression, or in hyphaema when blood cells may block the drainage angle and cause glaucoma.

Antibiotic – chloramphenicol (D.12.1) when there

is infection with pussy discharge, or an ulcer. Ointment stays around the eye and need only be put in twice a day, but it feels gooey and fogs the vision; instil drops at least every 6 hours. Antibiotics all have chemical preservative bases, which sting and cause irritation that can compound an existing problem.

Steroid – dexamethasone (D.12.1) has a magical effect on many red eyes but only skilled hands should use it because it delays healing and may rot the cornea in herpes virus infection.

Infection and inflammation – painful red eye(s)

INFECTION

Conjunctivitis:
usually both eyes feel gritty as though there is sand in them; they look red, may water and discharge, and resent bright light (photophobia). Vision is unaffected.
Treat: dark glasses. Most conjunctivitis is viral or allergic, so antibiotics will have no effect; only nature, time and patience will.

Corneal ulcer:
fluorescein shows up a stain, usually central and circular. Vision will be blurred if the ulcer lies dead centre of the cornea on the visual axis. Corneal ulcers are usually caused by bacteria, may take 1 to 2 weeks to heal, and rarely scar permanently.
Treat: mydriatic (D.12.3), antibiotic (D.12.1), dark glasses.

Herpes simplex:
a mature herpetic corneal ulcer may have squiggly, branching arms (dendrites), which stain with fluorescein. 'Kissing',

or 'cold' sores on the lips give away the diagnosis. Herpes is a virus, hard to diagnose without magnification, and difficult to treat. If someone with a red eye has had herpes before, presume it is herpes again.

Treat: mydriatic (D.12.3), [aciclovir] 3% eye ointment [zovirax] 5 times daily.

INFLAMMATION

Iritis:
usually a single eye becomes red, painful, photophobic and the vision is blurred. The pupil may be stuck to the lens, appears irregular, and is immobile in response to light. Iritis is difficult to diagnose even with magnification. A history of previous attacks should arouse suspicion.

Treat: mydriatic (D.12.3), steroid (D.12.2), dark glasses.

Contact lens keratitis:
contact lenses scratch the cornea causing painful inflammation. If the lens is left out the cornea usually heals in 24 to 48 hours. Tea will soothe meanwhile.

To remove a soft contact lens, moisten the tip of the finger, hold the lids open with the other hand, look down, and pinch it off with finger and thumb.

Eyelid cysts and styes:
occur as uncomfortable, red, swollen lumps on the lid margins, sometimes with a core of pus.

Act: try to pull out any lash that appears to arise from the centre of the lump. Apply heat by winding cloth round a wooden stick, dipping it in boiling water and holding it as close to the eye as possible without scalding the lid. Heat soothes and the cyst or stye may come to a head and burst. Antibiotics locally are to no avail.

Injuries

Subconjunctival haemorrhage:
a mild bang on the eye, or even rubbing it during sleep, can spill a single drop of blood that spreads out under the loose sheet of conjunctiva. The eye goes a horrifying scarlet, will change through all the colours of the rainbow and fade within 3 weeks. It is of no sinister import, provided the posterior limit of the blood is visible by turning the eye towards the nose; if in a serious injury with bruised and black eyes, no posterior limit is visible, suspect bleeding from the brain – a very serious sign.

Corneal abrasion:
caused, for example, by inturned eyelashes, a brush with a twig or pine needle, or a flying wood chip. The eye is very painful for 24 to 48 hours by which time most abrasions are healed; if pain persists more than 2 days consider an ulcer or infection.

Act: pluck out an inturned lash for instant relief. If the cause is otherwise, use tea.

Treat: mydriatic (D.12.3) and dark glasses, analgesic (D.1), antibiotic (D.12.1) if signs of infection.

Foreign body:
a speck of dirt or metal embedded in the cornea can often be seen with the naked eye. Sometimes it is lodged in the fornix of the upper or lower lid, or is stuck to the underside of the upper lid where it scratches with every blink.

Act: lie the person down to avoid fainting; then wash the eye with copious water.

Treat: local anaesthetic (D.12.4) 2 drops. Try to wipe the speck away with a folded corner of tissue. If it won't budge,

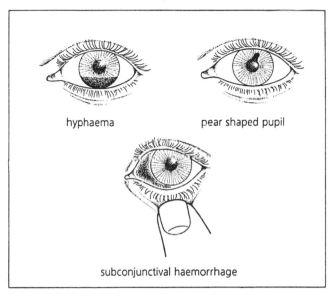

hyphaema

pear shaped pupil

subconjunctival haemorrhage

Eye injury

use a pushing motion with the end of a matchstick, approaching cautiously from the side to avoid digging into the cornea

mydriatic, tea; only use antibiotic if infection is evident.

After removing a metal foreign body, residual iron pigment often forms a ring of rust where the metal lay in contact with the cornea. A rust ring must be removed later by an eye specialist. Observe for perforation (see below).

BURNS

When the face is burned the lids take the brunt of the damage because blinking usually occurs before flame touches the cornea. Corneal burns may be caused by fire sparks, ultraviolet light and chemicals.

Ultraviolet burn (snowblindness):

Sun reflects strongly off snow and light-coloured rocks; its rays penetrate hazy cloud and become more powerful with altitude. The resulting ultraviolet burn of the cornea causes intensely painful inflammation with the eyes screwed up tightly. About 6 hours after a burn, swelling of the conjunctiva and blistering of the cornea make the victim temporarily 'blind', so he has to be led or carried to a lower camp, with all the attendant risks.

Act: prevention; wear goggles or dark glasses with side-shields to exclude glare. In emergency make horizontal slits or multiple pinholes in a piece of cardboard or duct tape doubled on itself, and tie it round the head with a piece of string, like Inuit snow goggles.

Treat: analgesics (D.1) and tea; local anaesthetic drops (D.12.4) will relieve pain and spasm long enough for the person to reach camp unaided and so may be life-saving. Do not use anaesthetic drops for prolonged pain relief. After reaching safety treat both eyes as severe corneal abrasions.

Chemical burns (caused by battery acid, or lime):

Act: wash the eye immediately and repeatedly with copious water for at least 5 minutes, and remove any lumps of chemical. Wash with bicarbonate of soda (baking soda) for acid burns, which usually heal quickly; milk or vinegar for alkali burns the consequences of which are often severe.

Treat: mydriatic (D.12.3), analgesic (D.1).

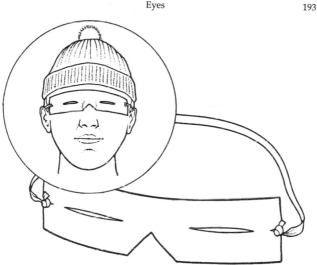

Snow goggles

BRUISING

After a blow on the globe of the eyes blood may completely fill the anterior chamber in the front of the eye, obscuring vision; after a few hours it settles forming a crescent. If the victim does not rest completely there is danger of more bleeding which seriously threatens vision.

Act: complete rest for 4 or 5 days. Patching the eyes has little effect on the outcome.

Treat: analgesics (D.1) and a sedative, lorazepam (D.5.1) make lying still easier. Do not dilate the pupil because blood may block off the drainage angle and cause glaucoma. Use tea only. If the eye remains inflamed after 4 days start steroid drops (D.12.2) every 6 hours.

Injury to the back of the eye (posterior chamber) is only visible with an ophthalmoscope, and is even more serious.

> *Bleeding into the vitreous;* vision is very blurred and no red background is visible with an ophthalmoscope, just a black reflection. *Retinal detachment;* a shadow may appear like a curtain falling across the vision, wavy shadows of matter floats around in the vitreous, and there may be a sensation of flashing lights.

Act: both conditions need an eye surgeon urgently. Patch the eye meanwhile and rest as much as possible.

High altitude retinal haemorrhage (HARH):
(see page 250)

OPEN INJURY (penetrating)

Infection and disorganization of the interior of the eye are hazards of penetrating injury. A wound may be seen across the cornea (less commonly the white sclera) but often the wound is tiny and seals over, disguising the mischief. Vision is reduced and the eye is red. The iris lies close against the back of the cornea. The pupil may be irregular and pear-shaped because part of the iris gets caught in the wound. To test for anterior chamber fluid touch a fluorescein paper strip on the upper part of the eye and observe closely for a streak of fluorescence dribbling down where eye fluid and dye mix.

Act: penetrating injuries are very serious and warrant an eye surgeon's urgent attention. Sympathetic inflammation in the opposite uninjured eye can occur within 2 weeks, and lead to blindness.

Treat: double dose of antibiotic cephalosporin (D.2.1) by mouth, analgesics (D.1), dark glasses.

EYELID INJURY

Always check the globe of the eye for associated injury. Eyelid repair requires surgical skill to restore accurately the windscreen wiper mechanism. Beware an injury in the corner of the eye near the nose where the tiny tear ducts may be torn; they need speedy repair.

Treat: antibiotic drops (D.12.1), pain-killers, and patch meanwhile.

FACIAL FRACTURE

The bony ring around the orbit may be disrupted so the eyeball sinks causing double vision (diplopia). The cheek is flattened and tender, and sometimes a step may be felt in the smooth lower rim of the orbit by running a finger along it.

Act: a pirate's patch eliminates diplopia until a surgeon can be reached.

17

EARS, NOSE, THROAT AND TEETH

Ears

FOREIGN BODY

Small round objects and insects may lodge in the outer ear. Hairs in the ear canal waft wax and junk towards the outside.

Act: pull back the earlobe to straighten the canal and to get a clear view of the drum. Lubricate the ear passage with a couple of drops of liquid paraffin or cooking olive oil. Turn the head on one side and shake vigorously. Gently flush the ear with clean, warm water using a syringe, pointing the nozzle towards the roof of the canal; 5 to 10 irrigations should allow the foreign matter to slide out. Do not dig for wax or poke around with matchsticks because you may damage the ear drum. If you see a foreign body in the canal try to pick it out with tweezers, or a thin wire loop manoeuvred past and then withdrawn.

AVULSION OF THE EAR

If an ear is torn off by a dog, or during a wild pub game, wrap it in chilled wet gauze and hurry off to a plastic surgeon. If merely torn, patch it together with Steri-strips, apposing the cut edges closely.

EUSTACIAN TUBE BLOCKAGE

When the tube leading from the back of the throat to the middle ear is blocked by swelling owing to a throat infection,

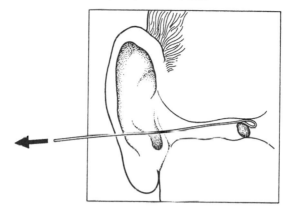

Foreign body in ear

or by sudden change in pressure such as in airplanes, hearing is dulled and the person feels like yawning to relieve the block.

Act: yawn, swallow hard or blow out against a closed nose, mouth and throat. Blockage usually clears in its own time. If obliged to fly when suffering from a cold, chew gum before take-off and landing.

Treat: phenlyephrine (D.14.1) decongestant nose drops and steam inhalation every 6 hours.

ACUTE MIDDLE EAR INFECTION (otitis media)
Searing pain develops in the affected ear, usually with high fever. Hearing is dulled. Fluid under pressure in the middle ear may rupture the eardrum and drain. A faulty upper wisdom tooth can cause earache.

Act: a light cotton-wool plug in the outer ear keeps out cold, which aggravates pain. Warm olive oil dropped into the ear soothes as does placing the ear against a hot-water bottle.

Treat: analgesics (D.1) and cephalosporin (D.2.1) by mouth.

LABYRINTHITIS

Virus infection in the middle ear may follow a cold; it upsets the balance so the person feels unsteady, nauseated and utterly miserable.

Treat: antihistamines (D.3) helps but is sedative, which may be an asset while resting. Time heals, but it may take 6 weeks.

MENIÈRE'S DISEASE

Severe vertigo causes the person to fall to the ground, vomit, and sweat profusely, followed by deafness and ringing in the ears – a most unpleasant combination. Reassure the person it will pass.

Treat: antihistamines (D.3) and restrict salt.

Mouth

MOUTH ULCERS

Aphthous ulcers (canker sores):
are painful and irritating.
Traumatic ulcers:
a rubbing tooth ulcerates the inside of the cheek.

Act: mouth washes of salt or baking soda. Gentian violet paint made from crystals heals mucosal surfaces but is mucky to use.

Herpes simplex:
contagious sores frequently accompany colds, especially at high altitude. Lesions on the lips, inside the nostrils, and (rare though much publicized) on the genitals form blisters which crust, scab and heal after 2 to 3 weeks.

Act: wash all eating utensils and cups carefully. Keep the blisters dry by dabbing with alcohol; refrain from kissing.

Nose

COMMON COLD

Colds are caused by viruses; runny nose, sore throat and fever usually clear within a week. Don't use antibiotics, which have no effect on viruses.

Act: avoid contagion by sleeping head-to-toe in a well-ventilated tent. Inhale steam with tincture of benzoin; gargle with 1 tsp of salt in 1 litre of water. Garlic cloves, chilli peppers, mustard plasters, or horse radish may help; give zinc tablets a try but don't waste money, space or energy on extra vitamins.

Treat: paracetamol (D.1.1), phenylephrine (D.14.1) nose drops. If a cold settles on the chest leading to bronchitis with yellow or green spit
    antibiotics (D.2).

SINUSITIS

Bacterial infection of the air sinuses around the face produces yellow or green snot often tinged with blood; also severe headache over the forehead or behind the eyes, and pain and tenderness over the cheek or brow overlying the sinuses, or in the upper teeth. Rarely frontal sinusitis spreads back to the brain causing meningitis.

Act: inhale steam to liquefy snot and shrink the swollen mucosal lining of the air passages, thereby encouraging drainage.

Treat: phenylephrine (D.14.1), antibiotics (D.2).

HAY FEVER (allergic rhinitis)

Hay fever causes nasal congestion with watery nasal discharge, itchy eyes and nose, and sneezing.

Treat: phenylephrine (D.14.1), antihistamines (D.3).

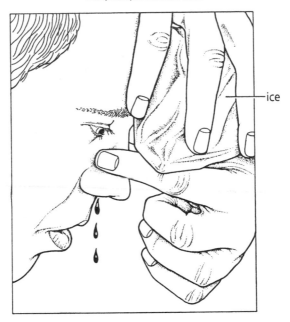

Stopping nosebleed

NOSEBLEED (epistaxis)

Ice and pressure alone usually stops bleeding after a few minutes, but rarely it may be uncontrollable, threatening life. Bleeding arises from the septum between the nostrils or high in the nose, well out of sight; it is never a safety valve, as folk-lore would have it, and may indicate high blood pressure.

Act: lean the person slightly forward with the head bowed. Encourage him to blow clots out of his nostrils; they do nothing to stop further bleeding and just dam blood that will trickle into the stomach and make him vomit. Identify from which side the blood is coming. Place a cold compress, preferably of ice or snow wrapped in a damp cloth, across the bridge of the nose. Squeeze the nostrils for 20 minutes below where the bone and soft nose cartilage join. Discourage breathing through the nose, picking at clots, blowing the nose, or sneezing, for 24 hours. If the air is very dry, as at altitude or in severe cold, apply vaseline to the affected side once the bleeding has stopped.

If bleeding persists push a gauze pack soaked in adrenaline (D.7.2) or phenylephrine (D.14.1) as high as possible up the offending nostril and leave it there for 24 to 48 hours. If bleeding starts again on removing the gauze, repack the nostril. Packing the post-nasal space via the mouth is fraught with hazard and should only be done by an expert. Sew 3 long strings of thread securely through a rolled gauze square. Pass a soft rubber catheter (or a Foley catheter, and blow up the balloon later) through the bleeding nostril, past the pharynx and out through the mouth. Tie 2 of the strings to the catheter tip and draw them back through the nose. Guide the pack up behind the uvula while pulling on the strings. Anchor the strings by tying them over a rolled gauze up against the nostril. Pull the third string out of the mouth and tape it to the face for removing the pack later (not more than 4 days).

BROKEN NOSE

A simple fracture with black eyes mars beauty; if associated with other facial fractures it may point to a serious head injury.

Act: ice reduces the swelling until a surgeon can deal with the fracture.

Throat

VIRAL SORE THROAT

Common virus infections cause a sore throat that looks fiery red; pus is absent, and the infection does not respond to antibiotics.

Act: gargle with warm salt water and suck throat lozenges.

TONSILLITIS OR STREP THROAT
Yellow flecks of pus lie on red, swollen tonsils; glands under the angle of the jaw swell and swallowing hurts.

Treat: cephalosporin (D.2.1), salt water gargles.

QUINSY
An abscess develops in the region of the tonsil bed, the soft palate swells and swallowing may become almost impossible.

Act: if medical help is far off, urgent, decisive lancing with a sterile blade into the most swollen part of the affected tonsil releases a gush of pus; this may be very difficult if the jaw is shut tight in spasm (trismus). Gargle with warm salt water.

Treat: cephalosporin (D.2.1).

HIGH ALTITUDE RAW THROAT
Breathing cold, dry air at high altitude is the cause.

Act: moisten the air by inhaling steam from a bowl, or sniff a billycan on the stove while making a tea brew, but don't scald your nose or throat. Usually lozenges are scarce on expeditions; drink lots of fluid and suck on hard candies instead.

GLANDULAR FEVER (infectious mononucleosis)
The person feels rotten, sluggish and washed out for no apparent reason. A thick yellow slough in the sore throat looks worse than it feels. Lymph glands in the neck, armpit and groin swell.

Act: rest (ideally for 4 weeks) because the disease can recur with activity; rarely an enlarged spleen can rupture. It may take several months before the person feels full of vigour again.

Treat: prednisone (D.4.1) if the throat swells and restricts swallowing and breathing.

SWALLOWED FOREIGN BODY

Eat dry bread to dislodge a fish or chicken bone stuck in the gullet. An immovable chicken bone will have to be taken to a surgeon. A piece of meat stuck in the gullet may threaten life – the Heimlich manoeuvre (see page 60) may dislodge it.

Emergency cricothyrotomy is rarely needed.

HICCOUGH

Distressing and unpleasant rhythmic reflex contractions of the diaphragm need interrupting.

Act: drink a cup of iced water fast (some try it standing on their head); hold the breath or breathe into a paper bag; press on the eyeballs, or tickle the back of the throat with a feather – all to stimulate the vagus nerve.

Teeth

TOOTHACHE

Toothache can disable a person totally; so have a careful dental check before setting off on an expedition, eat a diet with adequate vitamin C, and clean the teeth regularly. If without a toothbrush, rub the teeth with a moistened finger covered with salt, or with a peeled green stick. Sugarless chewing gum cleans the mouth, freshens the breath and exercises the gums.

Intense hot or cold causes pain in diseased or exposed teeth, especially at high altitude. Cold teeth may fracture suddenly when warmed by a hot drink or biting on hard food. Dental pain comes under many disguises, aching, throbbing, searing, and it may be difficult to localize to a particular tooth, especially in the early stages. Pain often affects adjacent teeth and may spread from the upper to the lower jaw and vice versa, but never across the midline. An amateur in the field can give only simple treatment to tide the victim over until he can see a proper dentist.

FINDING AN ACHING TOOTH

Tap the suspected tooth gently on the top and side with a metal instrument, preferably a blunt dental probe. A diseased tooth will hurt. Do not stick the point into the exposed cavity or into the softened exposed root. Cold and heat worsen pain in living teeth, although cold relieves discomfort in the early stage of a tooth abscess.

SINUSITIS

Pain from an infected maxillary sinus (the air space behind the prominence of the cheek) can mimic pain in the upper jaw, and is a common reason for faultily extracting healthy teeth. In sinusitis with pussy snot discharging from the nose, it hurts to press the cheek or knock with a finger; pain on both sides is unlikely to be dental.

COMMON CAUSES OF TOOTHACHE

Abscess:
pus forms round the root of a decaying tooth. The throbbing pain is partly relieved by clenching the jaw and then opening the mouth. The face and jaw swell, the breath stinks and pain is severe.

Act: hot salt mouth washes soothe, cleanse and encourage pus to discharge into the mouth.

Treat: cephalosporin (D.2.1), analgesics (D.1); extract the tooth only as a last resort.

Cavity:
a breach in the enamel due to decay, a lost filling or a fractured tooth, lays bare the sensitive inner dentine layer.

Act: use a temporary dressing of zinc oxide powder mixed with oil of cloves, or a synthetic tooth cement from a tube (stoppered to prevent hardening). Do not dig out any filling remnants with a pointed dental probe. Push the dressing paste into the hole with a finger and press it down with a matchstick.

Exposed tooth root:
when open to the cold, exposed roots cause pain which unattended may develop into chronic toothache.

Act: avoid heavy brushing and contact with very hot or cold.

MOUTH INFECTIONS

Bacterial:
(Vincent's infection, trench mouth) – poor oral hygiene allows plaques to grow next to the gums, which become infected, may swell painfully, bleed and ulcerate causing evil breath.

Act: use a toothbrush carefully. Gentian violet paint, made up from crystals, though messy to use, deals with most mouth ulcers.

Treat: antibiotics (D.2).

Pericoronitis:
Food debris collects under the gum flap over a partially erupted 3rd molar tooth. Infected gums swell and are further traumatized when pinched in chewing. Soon the person is unable to chew and the mouth is foul and painful.

Act: rinse vigorously with hot salt water. Reach under the flap into the crevices of the gum with a bent hypodermic needle, and flush out pus and debris with salt water.

Treat: antibiotics (D.2).

DISLOCATED OR AVULSED TEETH

Use warm salt mouthwash, replace tooth immediately in the socket and try to stabilize it. It may take like a free graft. If on the way to a dentist, store the tooth hamster-like in the person's cheek.

TOOTH EXTRACTION

If far from help, extracting a very painful tooth may allow the person, who would otherwise be an invalid, to continue with the expedition. Take out a tooth only as a last resort because skilful dentists can renovate some awful-looking teeth. The art of extracting a loose or a bad tooth can be learned easily enough, but to remove a strong, live tooth is very difficult. You need the proper tools, preferably some local anaesthetic, and a stoical patient. Before leaving on an expedition learn from a dental surgeon how to inject local anaesthetic.

Treat: antibiotics (D.2) before attempting extraction; local anaesthetic xylocaine 2% (D.17.1) with adrenaline 2ml for each tooth. If swelling is severe this may not help.

Upper jaw: insert the needle just through the skin where the gum and the cheek join, near the apex of the affected tooth. Put in a few drops to start freezing; after 2 minutes advance the needle and distribute the remainder of the 2ml around the tooth. Do the same on the palate side where there will be more resistance because of tight tissues.

Lower jaw: local anaesthetic placed as described above may be effective from the premolars forward. Behind the molars, a mandibular block is needed, which requires skill.

When the tooth is anaesthetized, or the patient is sufficiently drugged to allow the ordeal, grasp the tooth with a pair of upper or lower dental forceps. Push the beaks of the forceps down each side of the tooth below the gum margin to get a hold as far down the root as possible. Use a sideways rocking and rotating

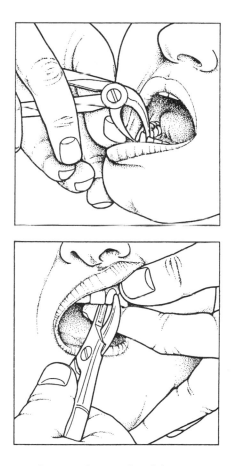

Lower and upper dental forceps

movement to work the tooth loose. The roots separating from the jaw make a disturbing crunch. If the tooth breaks, try to remove the remaining fragments, but do not dig deeply for them or the socket may bleed profusely. Pinch the gums together to stop bleeding and have the victim bite on a damp gauze pack or paper tissue for 15 minutes. If bleeding still will not stop pack the socket with gauze. Even removing the tooth crown alone may diminish the pain by letting pus discharge down the roots into the mouth. Smoking may restart the bleeding, so desist. Start hot salt mouthwashes on the second day.

18

COMMON GUT PROBLEMS

Hygiene

Water and food are the most common sources of disease because of pollution by infected faeces and urine of disease-carriers e.g. typhoid, shigella, cholera and hepatitis A – in short, you get ill from ingesting someone else's stool. People in tropical countries are generally less discriminating about where they defecate, partly owing to ignorance, partly to lack of adequate latrines. Food and drinking water become contaminated directly by faecal bugs, or shit-eating flies. To prevent disease drink only pure water, eat clean fresh food and dispose of sewage efficiently.

WATER

Hillside springs clear of human habitation and animal grazing should be safe for drinking, but stream and river water is probably polluted. Glacial mud and mica, which give alpine rivers their murky appearance, often upset the gut.

Outside Europe and North America consider all water, even in hotels and restaurants, unsafe to drink unless boiled; kitchens are probably only as clean as are the toilets. If in doubt about drinking water, purify it yourself and only drink boiled water, or tea or coffee made with boiling water. Avoid tap water, even for brushing teeth. Certain towns, e.g. Kathmandu, have notoriously polluted civic water supplies.

Water purification

Boiling:
the only way to sterilize water properly. Boiling briskly for
a few seconds kills most stool organisms; for 1 minute kills
amoeba cysts and hepatitis virus (even at high altitude
where the boiling point is lower than at sea level). The
colour, taste and smell of water is relatively immaterial,
provided it has been adequately boiled.

Chemical treatment:
chlorine and iodine (both halogens) kill most water-borne
bacteria and protozoa, but not amoeba cysts or bacteria
embedded in solid particles. They depend on concentration,
temperature and contact time of chemical to water. They are
available as:

Iodine:
– tincture of iodine or 2% Lugol's solution (5 drops/litre
for clear water, 10 drops for cold or cloudy water, allowed
to stand for 30 minutes)
– saturated iodine crystals; place a teaspoonful of iodine
crystals in a small glass bottle (wait 30 minutes when using
warm water, 1 hour if cold), decant the iodine-saturated
solution leaving the residual crystals behind, and keep top-
ping up with water to make more solution until all the
crystals have dissolved (N.B. ingesting the pure crystals
could be fatal). Add 1 to 2 drops of solution to a litre of
water and wait 30 minutes before drinking
– iodine tablets; add 1 tablet to 1 litre of water (but tablets
deteriorate over 6 months).

Chlorine:
– household bleach; add 2 drops to 1 litre of water
– Halozone tablets; add 2 tablets to 1 litre of water
It is not practicable to purify large volumes of water by

boiling. Use commercial chlorine or iodine bought across the counter. Treat the water for 30 minutes to 1 hour. A pinch of salt added to each litre improves the taste.

Filtration·
gives the water a deceptively clear appearance by removing suspended matter and some bacteria, but not viruses (which may be killed by an iodine exchange resin filter). Though useful for cleaning large volumes of water, filtration is the least reliable way of making it pure. Charcoal filters improve the taste and appearance of water but do not absorb all bugs. Filters have to be kept scrupulously clean or they lose their efficacy; they are bulky and expensive.

Boil water after filtration, not before. Filter cloudy water before treating with chemicals.

DRINKS
Bottled fizz, iced drink cubes and ice lollipops are only as safe as the water from which they are made. Boil unpasteurized milk; powdered milk is only safe if made up with boiled water and stored in a refrigerator. Wine in moderation is harmless but a surfeit upsets the stomach. Contrary to legend, alcoholic spirits do not sterilize the gut.

ICE CREAM
Ice cream harbours germs, both in the ingredients and from subsequent handling. Well advertised brands with a reputation at stake should be reasonably safe.

FOOD
Bacteria are killed by heat, so freshly and thoroughly cooked food should be safe. Avoid pre-cooked and handled food, especially where flies abound. Peel all fruit and vegetables; thorough washing is only second best, so beware of salads, tomatoes, lettuce and watercress because human night-soil

is often used as a fertilizer in the tropics. Meat should be thoroughly cooked and eaten immediately because raw or under-done beef and pork harbour tapeworms. Beware of inadequately cleaned prawns and shellfish, which live on sewage and concentrate the organisms.

Strike a balance between common sense precaution and worrying obsessively about what you eat and drink. Some early contact with germs and the accompanying dose of the runs is inevitable; immunity gained may protect against further attacks.

PERSONAL HYGIENE

Many toilets are dirty; squatters have to keep balance by holding onto the walls. Take toilet paper because newsprint is rough and fragile, and glossy magazines are impossible. Always burn toilet paper completely after use, before it becomes tree decoration along the trail. Wash hands carefully with soap and water immediately after shitting. Keep nails short and clean.

Gut ailments

DIARRHOEA

This causes more trouble than all other medical hazards encountered abroad. It has several forms and as many patent remedies as local names (Gippy Tummy, Delhi Belly, Kathmandu Quickstep, Tokyo Trots, Rangoon Runs, Montezuma's Revenge). The causes may include gluttony, change in climate and an upset in bacteria that are normal and necessary in the bowel.

Diarrhoea may arise from toxins, which are waste products of certain bacteria that grow on food (travellers' diarrhoea = food poisoning), or from infection by disease-causing bacteria carried in water and food (bacterial diarrhoea = dysentery) e.g. enterotoxigenic E. coli and shigella, less commonly with salmonella and other bacteria, protozoa and viruses.

Wise doctors recommend preventive hygiene before treating travellers' diarrhoea with drugs. Much pleasure in travelling abroad comes from eating local food and drinking wine; it's hardly worth going so far for beer, hamburger and hot dogs. But be moderate to avoid what could be a very expensive and distressing gut upset.

Travellers' diarrhoea (food poisoning):
is usually acute and self-limiting (lasting 6 to 12 hours), explosive and accompanied by vomiting. The gut is not actually infected, but poisoned with toxins instead, so treatment is purely supportive while waiting for the agony to pass, as it usually will quite rapidly.

Bacterial diarrhoea (dysentery):
starts suddenly (you'll remember the actual moment), and is distressingly uncomfortable with griping cramps often accompanied by vomiting, fever and bloody stools, sometimes also with slimy mucus and pus. The person may feel groggy because of dehydration from loss of body water. In extreme cases, especially when caused by shigella, the pulse rises quickly as does the temperature along with shivering rigors; you feel sick but usually do not vomit.

Protozoal diarrhoea:
starts gradually about 2 weeks after infection usually with churning upper abdominal discomfort, urgent crampy diarrhoea 5 to 6 times early in the day, rotten-egg burps and foul farts, but vomiting is rare. Diarrhoea developing weeks after return from abroad may be due to the protozoa Giardia lamblia.

Viral diarrhoea:
is rare and difficult to diagnose, so usually treated as if bacterial.
   Act: take frequent sips of fluid (at least 500ml an hour of

plain boiled water). If hungry, eat moderately; dried toast or peeled, grated apple turned brown (pecten) may help solidify the stools. A short period of starvation in a well-nourished person does no harm, but some shoestring travellers may already be malnourished so further starvation will not help.

The CIWEC Clinic in Kathmandu has unrivalled experience of treating travellers with diarrhoea and my advice is based on their protocol, which is more antibiotic-aggressive than was previously taught.

Antibiotics:
use with discretion because they kill normal, necessary bacteria as well as toxin-producers, they encourage antibiotic-resistant strains of E. coli to emerge, and they may prolong the excretion of bacteria during convalescence. However, that said, all pathogenic bacteria are killed by fluoroquinolone antibiotics – norfloxacin (cheaper and freer of side-effects) or ciprofloxacin.

Treat: (for bacterial diarrhoea) [ciprofloxacin] 400mg twice daily for 3 days. If severe diarrhoea (more than 6 stools per day) does not stop after 24 to 48 hours on this treatment, or if blood appears in the stools, go to a hospital for a stool examination. Generally speaking, co-trimoxazole, penicillins and tetracyclines are ineffective

Treat: (for protozoal diarrhoea) [quinacrine] 100mg 3 times daily for 5 to 7 days, if you can get it. Otherwise, metronidazole 250mg 3 times daily for 7 days (or [tinidazole] a single 2g dose daily for 2 days); it gives a metallic taste and doesn't mix with alcohol.

Fluid loss:
in severe diarrhoea with vomiting large volumes of water (and electrolytes) may be lost, causing rapid dehydration. Replace fluid according to the WHO formula (D.18), which can be made up by any pharmacist (see page 43).

Sip one glass (250ml) after each bowel movement, or more

if still thirsty or if the urine is scanty or yellow and concentrated. For less than 10 watery stools daily drink 1 to 2 litres every 24 hours; if more than 10, sip 1 to 2 litres every 6 hours. On an expedition abroad carry several packets of one of the commercial oral rehydration powders.

Bowel calming drugs:
slow the gut's contraction, and ease diarrhoea and cramping pains, but they may prolong bacterial illness by slowing excretion of bacteria and toxins. Most are related to narcotic drugs so may cause drowsiness. Do not use for more than 2 to 3 days.

Treat: codeine phosphate (D.1.3) 15 to 30mg every 8 hours and loperamide (D.9.3) 4mg every 8 hours; they can be given together.

Other medicines:
many popular brands of diarrhoea medicine are at best useless (Kaopectate alters the consistency of the stool and relieves discomfort for those who have to keep moving), at worst dangerous (iodohydroxyquin 'Entero-vioform' can cause blindness). Avoid them.
To prevent diarrhoea – in exceptional circumstances only – take [doxycycline], a long-acting tetracycline, 100mg daily for 3 weeks from the day before departure. It reduces your own bacterial flora and may increase the risk of more serious enteric infections.

CONSTIPATION

Not drinking enough is the commonest cause of this miserable state. Dehydrated foods worsen it and add to noisome gas. Eat a preventive diet of bran, cereal roughage, and fruit. If this fails use a laxative, mineral oil, bisacodyl (D.9.4) or a soap and water enema, in that order. Dehydration can turn the stools to concrete and ruin a trip (and may even require manual removal with a well-greased finger).

VOMITING

A stomach upset from dietary indiscretion or food poisoning may cause a short burst of vomiting, which usually settles in a day by stopping eating and taking sips of fluid only. If vomiting persists, suspect some more serious intra-abdominal mischief and seek medical help.

INDIGESTION

Stomach gas may cause a bloated, dyspeptic feeling behind the lower end of the breast-bone (sternum), or in the upper abdomen (epigastrium); it is often relieved by a hearty belch. The discomfort, colloquially called heartburn, may be so severe as to mimic the chest pain of a heart attack. Many healthy people have spent a night in intensive care wired to electronic monitors until cured by a glass of milk and a dose of antacid medicine. Farting may also cause a social problem, especially at high altitude.

Avoid heavy meals, but do not let the stomach lie empty for long periods because stomach acid starts to gnaw away at the lining, which is how ulcers start. Every 2 hours eat a biscuit with a glass of milk, which coats the stomach and gives the natural hydrochloric acid something to work on. Aspirin is very irritating and in a sensitive person one tablet may start a significant bleed (haematemesis). Avoid fried food, fats, spices, nicotine, coffee and alcohol, all of which stimulate gastric acid production. What pleasures remain?

Treat: aluminium hydroxide (D.9.1), the base of a multitude of antacids; the liquid form gives quickest relief but tablets are more convenient for the pocket and can be bought across the counter in many proprietary forms.

Simple indigestion may be difficult to distinguish from acid regurgitation, peptic ulcer, and gall-bladder disease. In every instance when far from help treat as above, and if the symptoms persist seek a doctor for a proper diagnosis.

ACID REGURGITATION

The lining of the gullet (oesophagus) does not take kindly to stomach acid; regurgitating waterbrash causes burning pain behind the sternum. This also occurs when a portion of the upper stomach slides into the chest through a gap in the diaphragm (hiatus hernia). Discomfort is worst when lying flat and may cause vomiting; it is relieved by sleeping propped up, and taking the precautions described above.

PEPTIC ULCER

Gastric or duodenal ulcers cause gnawing pain in the pit of the stomach coming on a couple of hours after meals, and only partially relieved by indigestion treatment. A history may reveal that the ulcer has been lying dormant for years, but then flares up under stress or unaccustomed eating and living. The danger is of a sudden, torrential, life-threatening bleed (haematemesis) or perforation (peritonitis).

Treat: aluminium hydroxide (D.9.1) and cimetidine (D.9.2) for at least a month even if symptoms subside.

CHOLERA

This rare disease is spread by faecally contaminated water and raw shellfish. Sudden onset of profuse, watery diarrhoea with cramps and collapse due to dehydration (sometimes within a few hours) in a known epidemic area is cause to suspect cholera. Fluids and electrolytes must be replaced urgently.

TYPHOID (ENTERIC FEVER) AND PARATYPHOID

Fever increases in spiky fashion over 1 to 3 weeks and may reach 40°C (104°F), accompanied by vague abdominal pain and cough. Constipation at first may, rarely, turn to bloody, pea-soup diarrhoea. Less common symptoms are headache, a flushed face and rose-coloured spots on the trunk. Eventually the victim becomes prostrate and desperately ill.

Treat: [ciprofloxacin] the drug of choice, 500 to 750mg every 12 hours for 2 weeks. [Amoxycillin] 2g every 6 hours, or co-trimoxazole (D.2.2) 2 tabs every 6 hours are other choices. Under medical supervision only, prednisone (D.4.1) 10mg every 6 hours for 1 week reduces symptoms and the likelihood of the dangerous complication of perforation of the bowel.

Parasites

AMOEBIASIS (Entamoeba histolytica)
Dysentery may develop gradually over a month but the majority of infected persons are asymptomatic carriers. At the start 3 to 4 loose, foul-smelling stools are passed daily, alternating every few days with normal stools; rarely this increases to a daily dozen with blood flecks, slimy mucus, painful straining and colicky pain on the right side of the abdomen. Liver abscess is a dreaded late complication but is usually not related to an attack of amoebic dysentery.

Treat: metronidazole (D.2.3) 750mg every 8 hours for 1 week.

WORMS

Worms are a chronic cause of ill health in the tropics and can be prevented by careful hygiene. They rarely have symptoms and never cause diarrhoea. Usually one dose of the appropriate drug cleans out the worm, the ova of which must be identified by microscopy of the stool.

Round worm (ascaris), thread or pin worm (enterobius) and whipworm (trichuris):
the worms, or part of them, may be seen in the stool. An itchy bum is sometimes the first warning of enterobius. Worms can mimic appendicitis, which is a rare disease in

natives of the tropics, so surgeons should go easy on the knife.

Treat: [mebendazole] 100mg twice daily for 3 days.

Hookworm (ankylostoma) and strongyloides:
larvae enter through abrasions on the feet so wear shoes in infected regions. Anaemia may result from heavy and chronic infections.

Treat: [mebendazole] 100mg twice daily for 3 days.

Tapeworm (taenia) and diphyllobothrium:
thrive in undercooked beef, pork and fish. Segments of the worm pass in the stool but the head remains attached to the gut and must be killed to prevent it growing into another worm.

Treat: [niclosamide] 2g in 2 doses an hour apart, while fasting.

Schistosomiasis (bilharzia):
the infective stage of this fluke lives in fresh water and enters the body through unbroken skin, so beware of drinking from, and paddling or swimming in, slow-flowing rivers or lakes. The veins of the bladder or intestine are its favourite haunt, so blood may pass in the urine.

Treat: [praziquantel] 40mg/kg as a single oral dose.

19

HYPOTHERMIA

Concerning heat control, regard the body as divided into a central core, which houses the vital organs (brain, heart, lungs, kidneys) and a surrounding shell (muscles, subcutaneous fat, skin).

Hypothermia is general cooling of the body core, occurring when more heat is lost than is gained. Frostbite is local freezing of the shell. Immersion injury occurs in water without freezing. Both hypothermia and frostbite may coexist but treat hypothermia first because it can be fatal. Hypothermia is worsened by wet-cold, exhaustion, anxiety, injury, drugs and alcohol. Wet and wind are a lethal pair that chill more than dry-cold.

Denizens of polar climates and high altitudes, aware of the dangers of cold, dress in warm protective clothing. Inuit, Tibetans, Andean Indians and barefoot Himalayan hillmen appear to adapt to cold and survive by intuition in their hostile environment. But, if careless, all these people can suffer the ravages of cold unless they practise common sense prevention.

Prevention

Plan carefully even the shortest outdoor expedition. If the weather changes, be prepared to abandon the original plan and take an easier, shorter route home. The measure of a good mountaineer is knowing when to turn around. Watch for early signs of hypothermia and act promptly to avert it. Gauge your objectives to the party's weakest member. Distance and speed of travel vary with terrain, weather, and load; walking too far too fast, carrying too heavy a load, and being cold, exhausted, hungry and demoralized, abet hypothermia.

Children and adolescents withstand cold less well than adults because their surface area is large in proportion to their weight, and generally they carry less subcutaneous fat. With less experience and smaller reserves of stamina and mental fibre, they tend to flag and give up hope unless strongly led. Women are better insulated than men by reason of curvaceous subcutaneous fat; but their smaller surface area and lower body weight cancel out this advantage.

Temperature control

The temperature of the body core, is preserved at the expense of the shell. A temperature-regulating centre in the brain senses changes in the temperature of blood flowing through it, and maintains a balance between heat gain and heat loss. Hypothermia occurs when more heat is lost than is produced.

A rise or fall in core temperature of 2°C causes noticeable symptoms; a drop of more than 6° to 7° can kill. Core temperature is measured with a special low-reading thermometer (below 35°C (95°F)) placed in the rectum – awkward in someone fully dressed. Mouth and armpit temperatures are initially inaccurate but never read less than true core temperature.

CONSERVING BODY HEAT

Insulation:
air and fat are poor conductors and therefore good insu-

lators. Wool, polypropylene and pile trap air in the interstices of the fibres, which do not collapse when wet, as does goose or eider down. Water is an excellent conductor and thereby destroys insulation. The more layers of clothing the better the insulation. The early Everest climbers reached over c8,500m (28,000ft) dressed in Norfolk tweed jackets and breeches dipped in water-repelling alum, several layers of Shetland wool pullovers and long wool stockings.

Windproof, waterproof fabrics prevent entrapped air being displaced, and also diminish convection, conduction and evaporation. Breathable fabrics allow some ventilation, but if the pores are large enough for air to pass through, water can do likewise. Coated nylon does not breathe, so water condenses on the inside of an outer garment and soaks the clothing underneath. Cotton jeans protect poorly against cold and wet. Sitting on a mattress or a rucksack insulates from the cold ground.

Blood vessel constriction:
smooth muscle in blood vessels of the shell, under reflex control, constrict in the cold, keeping warm blood in the core and preventing heat loss from the shell. Much heat flows from the head, armpits and groins where large blood vessels run, so these areas need special protection.

BODY HEAT LOSS

Convection:
air temperature alone is meaningless as a physiological measure of cold because wind speed determines the chill felt. On a windless, sunny day at −40°C (−40°F) you can walk about lightly clad, but the least puff of wind will send you scurrying for shelter. At 0°C (32°F) with a 65kph (40mph) wind, cold may be intolerable. Wet-cold feels much chillier than dry-cold because conduction and evaporation are increased. Wind displaces trapped air, battling the wind

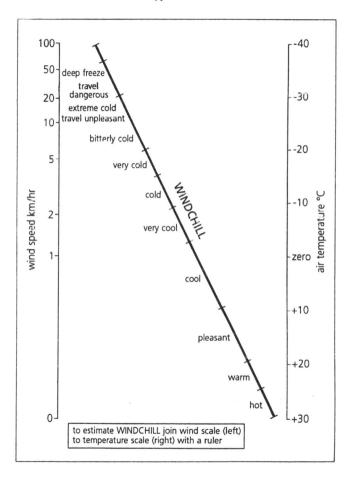

Windchill index

burns energy, and wind blowing on a wet surface increases evaporation. The windchill index is a graphic plot of wind speed against temperature. Windchill applies only to exposed skin and is irrelevant to persons wearing windproof clothing. It can give the wrong message, e.g. boating accident victims who do 20 times better out of the water clinging to an upturned boat, rather than staying submerged.

Convection also continues in the absence of wind because air warmed by skin rises away from the body. An uncovered head loses heat quickly – so when your feet are cold put on a hat. Wear a wool scarf, make a snug fit at the wrists with Velcro or elastic, and tuck trousers into socks or use gaiters. Mittens allow fingers to warm each other by mutual contact whereas gloves isolate each digit. For delicate touch, e.g. when handling a camera, wear silk gloves inside mittens.

Conduction:
heat flows by conduction directly from a warm body via wet clothes to the cold ground. Wind and wet reduce insulation of clothing ten times. Crossing glacial streams always wear long trousers for warmth, boots for sure footing, and belay securely with a rope. Legs immersed to the thigh cool fast, move slower and slower and may finally collapse, leading to drowning.

Evaporation:
to evaporate 1g of water requires 540 calories of heat. Body evaporation is caused by:
 – sweating: 0,5l (1 pint) of fluid normally evaporates daily through the skin – much more in hot climates and in dry-cold. During heavy exercise up to 1l may be lost each hour.
 – breathing: warm breath condenses in cold air and breathing cold air cools the airway. Much water can be lost during heavy breathing.

Blood vessel dilatation:

alcohol dilates blood vessels causing warm blood to flow away from the core to the periphery. Drunks found dead in snow banks sometimes have thrown off their clothes following a flush of warm blood that suffuses the body after the sympathetic nervous system finally breaks down. Alcohol makes a person less aware of cold, depresses heat production through shivering, and can cause a sudden fall in blood sugar (hypoglycaemia), especially when taken before exercise, because it depresses the mobilization of glucose from muscle glycogen stores. Alcohol is a serious potential hazard in the outdoors, but a nip of brandy may do wonders for the spirit of a cold, demoralized person.

BODY HEAT GAIN

Radiation:
sun and fire heat directly by radiation.

Exercise:
burns calories producing energy. Voluntary muscle work can produce up to 15 times the normal amount of body heat; involuntary shivering, 6 times. Exhaustion, alcohol and/or inadequate food or water decreases shivering.

Food:
metabolism of food produces energy that is converted into heat. An average sized adult male requires 4,000 calories each day for heavy work, equivalent to the energy consumed by walking around the Snowdon Horseshoe, 20km (12 miles), and climbing 750m (2,500ft). Carbohydrate is most quickly absorbed as sugar. Hot food and drink boost morale but transfer meagre heat to the stomach. Beware of eating snow to slake thirst; the same amount of heat is needed to melt snow as to bring that water to the boil.

Symptoms and signs of hypothermia

MILD HYPOTHERMIA: core temperature 37°C–33°C (98°F–91°F).

The person can usually still talk, but grumbles and mumbles about feeling cold, stiff muscles and cramps. Skin is cold, pale and blue-grey, owing to constricted blood vessels and sluggish circulation. Uncharacteristic behaviour may be obvious only to someone familiar with the person's previous personality and performance. Excitement, lethargy, poor judgement and decision-making are common features. Therefore never leave the person unattended, or allow him to wander off alone.

At a core temperature of about 35°C (95°F) he fumbles and stumbles because of poor muscular co-ordination. The brain is fuddled and he may hallucinate and shiver uncontrollably.

Act: the leader must decide whether to escape from the cold, wind and wet, or to stay put, shelter and summon help, which may take several hours to arrive. If the victim appears fit to go on, rest first. Shelter out of the wind, change out of wet clothes, eat some food and brew a hot, sweet drink. Boosted thus, he may be able to descend unaided. But don't sit around too long or he may cool further, as will his companions. Descend at his pace, not yours, to a camp or hut where he can be thoroughly warmed.

SEVERE HYPOTHERMIA: core temperature below 32°C (90°F).

Severe hypothermia is common in wet and cold environments especially in misadventures on mountains and on water. Shivering stops and thereby disappears the victim's last self-protective mechanism. His behaviour may be irrational and apathetic, or aggressive and violent. Muscle become stiff and movement is unco-ordinated, breathing slows and pupils dilate. He may have a seizure and slip into a coma. An irregular pulse heralds loss of control of the heartbeat. This all happens fast, and kills. The body core needs heat urgently during the first half hour after rescue.

Act: (on site)
Shelter:
the victim out of wind, rain and snow. Erect a tent, dig a snow hole, build a lean-to, or put him in a bivouac sack or a strong polythene bag. Insulate him well from the cold ground with a closed-cell foam mattress, rucksacks or foliage and grass. Once warm and dry, keep him that way.

N.B. Do not follow the former teaching to have a fit companion climb naked into a sleeping bag beside the unclothed victim, nor place against his skin a hot-water bottle, heated stones wrapped in cloth, or commercially produced 'heat-packs'. All these devices may stop him shivering, which is his safest way of rewarming.

Other members of the party may also be cold and miserable, and will need sustenance for the long, hard job of rescue. Crowd into a shelter, light a stove and brew a drink. Even a single candle will warm a small enclosed space, but beware of stoves producing poisonous carbon monoxide gas.

Leave at least one person to look after the victim. Send the strongest competent member of the party for help, having agreed on a signal to direct arriving rescuers to the victim. Write down the map reference and send it together with a written message about the condition of the victim. Radios and helicopters have greatly simplified modern rescues.

Having decided to stay put and shelter, do not waver even if the victim improves; by starting down he may relapse and you may miss the rescuers. If you have to descend because help is unavailable, plan an escape route that avoids ridges and windy places. If forced to carry him immobile on a stretcher, wrap him well because he may continue to cool, and remember that making a hypothermic person walk will further exhaust him.

If the victim is on a stretcher handle him very gently to avoid triggering lethal heart irregularities (arrythmias), and carry him head slightly downhill to maintain his blood pressure. One person should watch him closely all the time. Ideally, start i/v fluids before the evacuation begins.

Warm, humidified air breathing:
rewarming can be started in the wilderness with a portable apparatus that provides heat transfer directly to the core via the big blood vessels of the neck and chest; it also prevents further heat loss from expired air. Such first-aid treatment in the field is a useful adjunct to adequate body insulation.

One system (Lloyd) generates heat and moisture by passing oxygen through soda-lime previously charged with a pre-set volume of carbon dioxide. The temperature and humidity depend on the volume of carbon dioxide added.

In another system (U-Vic Heat Treat) air or oxygen passes through a heater-vaporizer unit at 70°C and into a reservoir re-breathing bag attached to a mask.

At base camp

Ideally an hypothermic victim should not be actively rewarmed until under total physiological control in hospital. But in a wilderness hypothermic incident it may be several days before such ideal circumstances are obtained. Therefore allow the person to rewarm slowly at his own pace in a sleeping bag without applying external heat. The danger of this period is of rewarming shock due to the sudden return of cold blood to the core carrying with it toxic metabolites of blood pooled in the cold shell.

Rewarming shock:
blood pressure falls and pulse rises above 160 per minute and is irregular – it can cause fatal irregularities (arrythmias) of the heart (ventricular fibrillation) and CPR may be necessary. Arrythmias are very difficult to diagnose in the field; all are bad news, especially in someone who is unconscious, under the age of 10 years or over 70, or has a history of heart disease.

Fluid replacement:
all hypothermics are short of fluid (dehydration), so give lots of fluid by mouth provided the victim is conscious. Hot bath rewarming worsens dehydration and shock by shunting blood from core to shell.

> If fluid is available give 1 to 2 litres of Ringer's lactate or normal saline immediately, depending on size. Follow this with 5% dextrose water (500ml every 6 hours) to help transfer glucose across cell membranes and to move potassium back into the cells. Place the i/v bag under his bum to build a head of pressure, warm the fluid and prevent it freezing. Give sodium bicarbonate (50 mEq in 50ml = 1 ampoule) in the first bag of fluid to neutralize any acidity of the blood.

Other rewarming methods are possible only in a well equipped hospital:

Peritoneal dialysis:
flushing warm dialysate fluid round the peritoneal cavity provides heat directly to the core and helps the body fluid equilibrate with the dialysate.

Extra-corporeal rewarming via cardio-pulmonary by-pass:
provides total control and is ideal for the desperately ill,
severely hypothermic patient.

DEEP HYPOTHERMIA

At temperatures below 28°C (82°F) a person may appear
dead; shivering is absent, muscles are stiff like rigor mortis,
skin is pale and bloodless, and heartbeat and breathing are
barely perceptible. But although oxygen for the brain and
heart is greatly diminished, it may be adequate for that temperature.

Declare a victim of hypothermia dead only *when warm and
dead*, i.e. if he has failed to revive after adequate rewarming.
A severely hypothermic victim who is still alive may have
fixed and dilated pupils, a common sign of death. The only
sure signs of death are no response when the victim is
rewarmed, and ECG evidence of the heart having stopped.
So do not give up too readily; 'corpses' have been known
to wake up in a warm mortuary.

IMMERSION HYPOTHERMIA

Immersion hypothermia differs from outdoors exposure in
its rapid onset and even faster cooling when exercising (e.g.
swimming). Heat is lost 25 times faster in water than air
because water is an excellent conductor. The victim may
drown because hypothermia causes loss of consciousness.

Volunteers, lightly clothed, floating motionless, immersed
to the neck in calm water will reach 'incipient death' in 2½
to 3 hours at 10°C (50°F), in 2 hours at 5°C (41°F), and in
1½ hours at 0°C (32°F). Rough seas shorten survival, but
protective clothing prolongs it.

A person can swim less than 1km in water at 10°C, (50°F)
so it will usually be safer to stay with an upturned boat
than to strike out for shore. Crouching in a foetal position
minimizes heat loss from thermogenic areas of the axilla and

groin, and limits burning calories in fruitless attempts at swimming to keep warm. A personal flotation device (PFD) prolongs survival threefold. Wool insulates better than any other normal clothing when wet. Covering the head reduces heat loss by half. It is warmer out of the water clinging to an upturned boat, despite wind and rain, than staying immersed. Staying with the boat increases the chance of being spotted by searchers. Despair is the overwhelming emotion of a shipwreck victim, who is inclined not to bother with details of survival skills that can tip the balance from death to life.

NEAR DROWNING

Panic and violent struggle to reach the surface is followed by a period of calm and breath-holding. Swallowed fluid causes vomiting, aspiration and gasping breathing. Finally the victim convulses, is comatose and looks like death.

Salt and fresh water affect the lungs differently, but the practical management of near drowning is the same.

Speed of restoring oxygen to a brain deprived of it by immersion in water can make a significant difference to the final outcome. You must clear the airway, pump in oxygen and restore the circulation of a stopped heart, but remember that all the major organs may have been affected by the insult. But do not endanger yourself or others in your keenness to help, or you may end up with two victims instead of one.

Act: start immediate mouth-to-mouth resuscitation (see page 57) wherever the victim is found, floating in water or beside a pool. Do not waste time trying to remove the victim to dry land; every second counts in minimizing brain damage.

To assess the victim properly, and to do CPR, remove him to a firm surface out of the water, but only after you have started ventilating his lungs. Over half of all near-drowning victims vomit during resuscitation, so do a finger sweep to clear the airway of solid matter, and place him in the rescue position whenever possible.

Remember the possibility of a neck injury in an unresponsive victim of a falling, diving or surfing accident. Someone submerged for more than one hour in normal temperature water will be dead.

Prevention:
teach swimming, especially to children. Insist on personal flotation devices (PFDs) whenever on water. Alcohol and watersports are a deadly combination.

20

FROSTBITE

Frostbite is localized freezing injury of the body shell, commonly of face, hands and feet. Hypothermia, by contrast, is generalized cooling of the core; it contributes to and may co-exist with frostbite. In severe cold weather if the core remains warm the extremities are less likely to freeze. Once frostbitten a person seems more susceptible to frostbite again in the same area owing to local nerve damage. Cold deserves profound respect because frost bites the unwary causing devastating disability.

After an accident damaged tissue freezes, especially if the victim is immobile from pain and unable to produce heat by exercise. Also, if the victim is unconscious, shivering may quit. Blood loss from an open wound or into a closed fracture causes clinical shock, and fear compounds emotional shock; in both events vessels in the extremities constrict to shunt blood from the limbs to the core to maintain vital functions with increased risk of frostbite.

At high altitude frostbite is hazardous because there is less oxygen to nourish the tissues. Over 6,000m (20,000ft) work is exhausting, sleep elusive and the brain dull – hence we forget common sense precautions against cold.

Prevention

BODY PROTECTION

A windproof, waterproof suit protects against hypothermia which cools the body core causing danger of frostbite in the extremities.

FEET

Tight boots cramp the circulation and cause blisters, which are liable to infection. Stop and remove boots as soon as the feet feel cold or begin to lose sensation; early warming may prevent trouble later. Windproof trousers keep the legs warm – and hence the feet; gaiters keep out snow. A wrinkled sock in a boot causes uneven pressure and inter-feres with blood flow. Carry spare dry socks, to double as mittens.

A plastic bag pulled over the foot next to the skin makes a vapour-barrier liner, which traps the warm moisture of sweaty feet keeping socks dry. At $-40°C$ ($-40°F$) and zero humidity the feet are quite comfortable and, surprisingly, it doesn't feel like standing in a swamp. Rubber vapour-barrier boots are very warm but bulky – good for plodding round camp, but clumsy for technical climbing. Plastic double-skinned climbing boots are warm, waterproof and do not freeze as do leather boots.

HANDS

Outer mittens allow fingers to move freely and to warm each other by contact, whereas gloves isolate each finger. Clothed hands still need to handle equipment like ropes, ice axes, and crampon straps. In severe cold get in the habit of doing all routine tasks wearing mittens because each time they come off, hands cool quickly. Silk or polypropylene gloves enable performing delicate manual tasks like hand-ling cold metal. Elastic cuffs of jackets and mittens should

be loose. Skin sticks to freezing metal so beware of metal
spoons and mugs, and never touch metal with your lips or
tongue.

FACE

The face is difficult to cover completely, even with neoprene
face masks; ears and noses cool fast because of their large
skin area. Carry a pocket signal mirror to inspect cheeks and
nose frequently for painless white patches of frostnip. A
balaclava wool hat with a visor protects most of the face. A
scarf tied loosely over the mouth and nose soon ices up with
frozen breath forming a barrier to the cold air. Breathing
very cold air can cause wheeze like asthma, and if prolonged
can damage the terminal air sacs ('frozen lung').

GENITALS

Men have the bigger problem. Fortified underpants, a rabbit
skin or newspaper stuffed down the front will keep everything warm. Once nipped, dipping in brandy does not
help.

Mechanism of frostbite

Fluid within the cell freezes, the nucleus bursts and the cell
dies; on rewarming, toxic breakdown products cause further
tissue damage. Small arteries in the shell constrict, so warm
blood flows to the core at the expense of the extremities,
which freeze. Capillaries are damaged by freezing and leak,
causing blisters. Cold red blood cells sludge and clot in the
small vessels preventing oxygen reaching the tissues.

   Climbers at high altitude are often stormbound in their
tents; without exercise they cannot stimulate circulation, and
they fail to drink enough because fuel for melting snow is
scarce. Oxygen lack causes red blood cells to multiply and
blood becomes viscous and sluggish. Small clots form in the

leg veins, pieces (emboli) break off and lodge in limbs and lungs.

Symptoms and signs of frostbite

Frostbite behaves like a skin burn; it may be superficial or deep, depending on whether the germinal layer of the skin (from which new cells arise) is damaged. Depth of freezing depends on temperature and length of exposure to cold.

SUPERFICIAL FROSTBITE

Superficial freezing (frostnip) damages only the surface cells, so expect complete healing without loss of tissue. Frozen tissue is white, waxy, and feels intensely cold, but it is soft and resilient when pressed. The skin tingles and is painful, indicating nerves are undamaged. Blisters may form.

Act: to get warm jump up and down, wriggle toes, flex ankles, clap hands and swing arms. Put a cold hand in your own armpit or crotch; pee on your fingers. Place a cold foot against the warm trunk of a fit, sympathetic companion. Hold a warm hand against numb ears or nose, or ask a friend to breathe on them. Never rub snow into a frozen part because snow crystals act like broken glass. Rubbing the skin vigorously may break the surface, encouraging infection. Numbness wears off as the part thaws, giving way to excruciating burning pain.

Treat: strong analgesics (D.1.3 or 4).

DEEP FROSTBITE

Deep freezing kills tissue and nerves with insidious loss of pain and cold sensation. Skin forms blisters and turns a mottled blue. Muscle may be frozen, but tendon is usually spared. Frozen tissue feels solid to touch, but frostbitten limbs can still move. The ugly appearance of frostbite, ranging from a patch of black skin to apparent gangrene of the whole limb, is a poor guide to how much tissue will die eventually – so be not hasty with the knife.

Act (on the hill): rest the frozen limb and keep it clean. Cells at the edge of an area of frostbite are balanced precariously between life and death and deserve mollycoddling to ensure they survive. Do not risk infection by pricking blisters. Cover the wound with a plain, dry, non-stick dressing, and splint the limb. Dead slough will usually separate from healthy tissue in 2 to 3 months, provided there is neither infection nor further damage.

A deeply frozen limb swells, feels tight and is difficult to move. Elevate the limb above body level to let oedema fluid drain away. Once a limb is thawed, keep it warm, at rest and protected from further injury. It is better to walk with feet still frozen before rewarming them, because thawing and refreezing does more damage than walking on frozen feet. A rewarmed and thawed person should preferably be carried on a stretcher. Blisters will break anyway while walking, so drain them with a sterile needle, then dress them cleanly. In remote regions the victim will have to rest at night and rewarming is inevitable. Do the best you can.

Act (in the valley): a frostbitten person may also be hypothermic. On reaching shelter or base camp, warm him thoroughly and make him comfortable. Give plenty of fluids. A wee dram of spirits will cheer, but forbid smoking because nicotine narrows small arteries by half. Treat pain and anxiety; then thaw the limb.

Thawing:
rapid thawing is less damaging to frostbitten tissue than slow rewarming; the limb is frozen for a shorter time and swelling subsides more quickly. Ice formed between cells melts and salts migrate, upsetting cell chemistry. Stagnant blood starts to recirculate carrying away poisonous chemicals formed during thawing.

Rapid thawing can only be done at a base camp where

adequate fuel and large containers of water are available. Immerse the frozen limb for 30 to 40 minutes in water at about 42°C (105°F) which feels pleasantly warm to the uninjured hand; using a thermometer is preferable. Hotter water boils tissue. A frozen limb cools the water bath so stir in more warm water frequently. Do not heat the bath directly. Never thaw a limb in front of an open flame as the flesh may cook. Continue thawing until the warmed tissue is soft, pliable, and flushed red. Pain may be severe (see below).

Cleaning and dressing:
after washing your own hands thoroughly with soap and boiled water clean the frostbitten area daily with a saline solution made with a tablespoon of salt in a litre of boiled water. Gentle dabbing is sufficient; do not scrub the skin surface. Separate fingers or toes with dry cotton wool.

If possible leave the frozen part open to the air to allow a scab to form. But do not be tempted to pick at the underlying healing tissue which needs nurturing like a seed bed. Take scrupulous care to avoid infection which will convert a dry healing scab into soggy, inflamed, wet gangrene that spreads up the limb destroying as it goes. If the wound has to be dressed use a [sulpha cream], and change the dressing at least daily. Exercise the part continually to prevent contracture of joints.

Treat: co-trimoxazole (D.2.2) broad spectrum antibiotic, especially if the line between healthy and dead tissue becomes inflamed. Double the dose if it looks red and inflamed, feels tender and throbs.

Morphine (D.1.4), or codeine (D.1.3) for pain.

Tetanus toxoid – get a booster dose as soon as possible.

Medical sympathectomy: [phenoxybenzamine] 10mg twice daily for 6 days may combat vasoconstriction.

Vasodilators [Ronicol, Priscol]. These drugs used to be fashionable with climbers but have no place in the field treatment of frostbite. They dilate vessels giving a deceptively pleasant feeling of warmth as blood surges to the skin surface; much heat is lost thereby with further damage of hypothermia and they do nothing for the frostbitten part.

HOSPITAL

Sympathectomy (surgical): may help if done in the first 24 to 48 hours after freezing.

Fasciotomy: should be done early to relieve oedema causing pressure on small vessels to the hands or in muscle compartments.

Amputation: wait for natural separation. Frostbite in January may mean amputation in July – not before.

Eschew heroic surgery in the field; spreading gangrene is the only indication for emergency amputation. Guess generously at the extent of irreparable damage; notoriously evil-looking limbs can, and do, recover almost completely.

Other types of cold injury

IMMERSION TRENCH FOOT

A non-freezing cold injury caused by prolonged exposure of many days, or even weeks, to cold and wet. Mild numbness and a feeling of never being warm may progress to freezing cold injury (frostbite).

CHILBLAINS

Repeated exposure of bare skin to wet, wind, and cold, cause red, itchy, tender, swollen skin.

21

HIGH ALTITUDE PROBLEMS

Acclimatization

Acclimatization is the physiological process that allows humans to adapt so they can live and work in the oxygen-thin atmosphere of high altitude. Life would be more difficult above about 10,000 feet or 3,000 metres without the physiological adjustments of acclimatization, which compensate for the low pressure of oxygen in the air (hypoxia), and high altitude mountaineering would be nearly impossible. Certainly no unacclimatized person could climb to the top of Mount Everest, or even survive there, without oxygen, a feat now achieved many times by well-trained, acclimatized mountaineers.

Our planet is surrounded by a diaphanous mantle of atmosphere, the gases of which exert pressure on the surface of the earth. The air we breathe at sea level contains four parts of nitrogen, to one part of oxygen. As we climb, the 4:1 ratio of these gases does not change, but their density becomes less; fewer molecules are present in a given volume of air and the pressure exerted by them falls steadily. Thus an ordinary weather barometer can be used as an altimeter because it registers the pressure gases exert on the earth.

At the top of Mount Everest (8,848m/29,028ft) the atmospheric pressure is about one third of that at sea level. The atmosphere is thinner over the North and South Poles, where the pressure is lower for any given altitude than over the equator. Eventually, as we climb, the pressure will no longer be adequate to drive sufficient oxygen from the air into the blood and thereby into the tissues, especially the brain.

Low oxygen pressure in the atmosphere, and hence in the lungs and blood, increases the rate and depth of breathing. Initially the heart beats faster and more strongly, increasing the flow of blood to the lungs, and breathing deepens and quickens; but this soon settles back to normal. Bone marrow at high altitude produces more red cells and haemoglobin, which allows blood to carry more oxygen. The blood becomes more viscous, or sticky, and the circulation is sluggish because the volume of blood plasma falls. This is partly because more urine is passed, partly because of dehydration caused by sweating with heavy exercise and by overbreathing in the cold dry atmosphere, and partly because the expanding red cell mass takes space at the expense of plasma volume.

THE INITIAL RAPID PHASE OF ACCLIMATIZATION

Breathing:
at sea level the rate and depth of breathing are controlled by the level of carbon dioxide waste produced by body tissues burning oxygen. Above 3,000m (c10,000ft) carbon dioxide control is over-ridden by the paramount need to get enough oxygen. Low oxygen pressure in the atmosphere, and hence in the lungs and blood (hypoxia), increases the rate and depth of breathing so carbon dioxide levels in the blood fall briskly until a steady state is reached for that individual at that altitude.

Breathing rate increases because hypoxia triggers the carotid chemoreceptor organs in the neck to stimulate the respiratory centre in the brain. With deeper breathing carbon dioxide, which dilutes oxygen in the lungs, is removed more rapidly; its concentration in the blood falls, which in turn dampens the activity of the respiratory centre. A delicate balance is struck between two opposing forces, low oxygen and low carbon dioxide pressure, which control the rate and depth of breathing.

Increased ventilation of the lungs, especially on exercise, provides more oxygen for absorption by the capillaries. On the other hand, at altitude the accessory breathing muscles (diaphragm, abdomen, intercostals and neck) burn more oxygen, so less is available for the hard work of climbing. Low carbon dioxide makes the blood more alkaline and, to compensate, more bicarbonate is excreted by the kidneys.

Cheyne-Stokes periodic breathing:
breathing rhythm commonly changes at altitude, particularly at night; it steadily deepens, rises to a crescendo, then falls off and finally ceases completely for several seconds. Then the pattern starts over again. Carbon dioxide in the blood builds to a level where it stimulates the respiratory centre. Breathing restarts, carbon dioxide is blown off, the stimulus lessens and breathing comes to a standstill. With acclimatization this abnormal behaviour of the respiratory centre settles down to a new level of stimulation by carbon dioxide.

Heart:
the heart beats faster and more strongly, increasing blood flow (cardiac output). The person feels thumping palpitations in the chest and a dull headache throbbing in time with the pulse. Hypoxia stimulates both the carotid chemoreceptors and the sympathetic nervous system, making the heart pump more blood to the lungs. Thereby more oxygen is available to the tissues where it is readily released because of the relative difference in pressure between blood and tissue cells. Many capillaries open to carry more blood to the cells. Pressure in the pulmonary artery rises so lung capillaries are better perfused and the surface area for gas exchange is increased.

THE LATE SLOWER PHASE OF ACCLIMATIZATION

Blood and plasma:
soon after arriving at altitude the volume of plasma, the fluid in which blood cells are suspended, falls by 20 to 30%. This is partly because more urine is passed at altitude, partly because of dehydration caused by sweating with heavy exercise, by overbreathing in the cold dry atmosphere, and partly because of a proven shift from the extracellular to the intracellular space. Water losses are hard to replenish above the snow line because fuel is scarce for melting snow to provide the normal daily requirement of 4 to 5 litres of water, and stoves work less efficiently at altitude.

Hypoxia stimulates bone marrow to produce more red cells in proportion to the severity of oxygen lack. As a result more haemoglobin is produced to carry more oxygen. At high altitude blood can carry up to half as much oxygen again as at sea-level. As red cells increase and plasma diminishes, blood becomes more viscous putting a greater strain on the heart. The circulation becomes sluggish, reducing oxygen delivery to the tissues. Red cells clump forming clots and stack together lessening the surface area for oxygen diffusion. Blood vessels in the calf muscles of stormbound climbers lying inactive in their tents fail to compress the leg veins which should normally pump blood efficiently back to the heart; the veins may clot, and some unlucky people even suffer strokes thereby.

Tissues:
blood is shunted from non-essential to vital tissues (brain, heart, and lungs). Adaptations in the cells assist the release and uptake of oxygen by mitochondria, the power units of cells. Several complex physiological changes assist more efficient use of oxygen; new capillary formation, increased muscle myoglobin and the enzyme cytochrome oxidase.

Acclimatization changes have one common purpose: to make optimum use of what little oxygen is available in the thin air on high. But ironically some of these adaptations defeat their own ends, for example, the blunted response of Sherpas to hypoxia.

Acclimatization is quite idiosyncratic; it starts at different altitudes and proceeds at different rates in different people. Some are never troubled provided they ascend slowly enough, while others for no obvious physical reason never acclimatize properly however long they remain high, even at relatively low altitude. It is not progressive. After about three months at very high altitude, say above 6,000m (c20,000ft), the climber steadily deteriorates. He sleeps and works poorly, and loses appetite and weight. Retreat to the valleys for a long holiday is the solution.

Acute Mountain Sickness (AMS)

Acute Mountain Sickness (AMS) is caused by diminished oxygen pressure in the atmosphere and hence in the blood (hypoxia), and strikes those who fail to adapt to high altitude, above 2,500m (c8,000ft). Anyone venturing into the high, cold, thin air is wise to study AMS, which can kill the unwary, the bold and the previously healthy. It affects those who ascend too high too fast, and is usually cured by immediate descent.

Mild AMS has vague, ill-defined symptoms but can drift subtly into severe AMS, which can kill. Hypoxia sets off a chain of events, the fundamental problem being that body water settles in the wrong places; the brain in High Altitude Cerebral Oedema (HACO); and/or the lungs in High Altitude Pulmonary Oedema (HAPO), or the tissues of the face, hands and feet.

N.B. North Americans spell edema for oedema and use the acronyms HAPE and HACE in common medical parlance.

Mild AMS

Many people who climb high (over 2,500m/c8,000ft) are fit on arrival but feel ghastly over the next couple of days, with headache, breathlessness, insomnia, fatigue, poor appetite, nausea and dizziness. As they adapt to the low partial pressure of oxygen in the air, these symptoms usually pass off. But some climbers never get used to the altitude, their symptoms become worse and worse, and some die from HACO or HAPO.

PREDICTING AMS

No one can predict who will suffer from AMS, whether it will be mild or severe, or when it will strike. Climbers who have performed well at altitude will probably do so again each time they go high. Those who have suffered AMS before may suffer again and at a similar altitude. Fitness and training guarantee no protection, the sexes succumb equally and no age is exempt. Weight gain during ascent means water retention, which bodes ill.

PREVENTING AMS

Allow ample time at various levels to acclimatize. AMS is more likely to occur the higher, the faster, the harder, and the longer the climb. Cold and wind, fear and fatigue, dehydration during rapid ascent and strenuous exercise soon after, and upper respiratory infection all predispose to AMS.

Climb without haste:
above 4,000m, (c13,000ft) gain height slowly and steadily at about 300m (c1,000ft) a day and take a rest day every 1,000m (c3,000ft). Avoid strenuous exertion soon after arriving at altitude. Carry expedition loads high; dump them, descend and sleep low. Keep loads light and rest frequently. High mountains should be approached at a leisurely pace both

for pleasure and safety; the first Everest climbers always did
so on their march through Tibet. They achieved Herculean
feats, reaching over 8,500m (28,000ft) in the early 1920s with
primitive equipment and clothing, and oxygen apparatus
which they rarely used because it was so heavy and clumsy.

Drink sufficient fluid:
4 to 5 litres, about 16 to 20 cups daily; this should balance
the heavy fluid losses caused by strenuous breathing in cold,
dry, thin air, and allow peeing a clear, colourless, copious
urine (1 litre daily, about 2 bursting bladder-fulls, is the
minimum acceptable). Dark yellow urine is concentrated,
usually indicating dehydration; it may however be part of
the water retention of AMS. Avoid alcohol; a hangover mim-
ics AMS and may confuse the diagnosis.

Eat a high calorie diet:
with plenty of carbohydrate before and during ascent. A
good appetite suggests good acclimatizing. Don't take salt
or sedatives.

If, despite these precautions, a climber gets sick and does
not improve on rest, descend quickly until he starts to feel
better. Even 300m will help; 1,000m may be magical and
life-saving. If the person feels ill and does not improve
quickly on descent, insist that he does not reascend on that
expedition.

Beware the climber who acclimatizes poorly and copes
less well than expected for the altitude and his previous
performance. Macho types who battle ever upward despite
worsening distress are those likely to end up buried under
a cairn of stones on the glacier.

SIGNS OF MILD AMS

These develop 12 to 48 hours after arriving at altitude.

Headache:
the person's head feels tight, and he may feel giddy and light-headed. Headache, usually at the back of the head, often develops during the night so is present on waking. If headache persists after exercise and taking 2 paracetamol tablets the person must descend. The severity of headache and its response to treatment is often a measure of the severity of AMS, yet some people are found unconscious in the morning without any warning.

Fatigue:
tiredness usually passes off with rest, fluids and food, all of which restore normal energy.

Appetite loss, nausea and indigestion:
a listless, sick, belching and farting tentmate is odious; but gas problems improve with acclimatization.

Sleep disturbance:
difficulty in falling asleep, and frequent waking occur in the first week but may improve in the second. At great height it may never improve.

Shortness of breath on exertion (dyspnoea):
the chest feels uncomfortable and tight, but quiet easy breathing resumes after rest. A raspy cough, caused by the cold dry air, is relieved by inhaling steam from a boiling pot.

Cheyne-Stokes periodic breathing is particularly noticeable and worrying at night.

Shortage of fluid (dehydration):
urine output is low for 24 hours with a story of not drinking enough and perhaps of exposure to heat and sun. Thirst rages, mouth lining and tongue are dry (also caused by mouth breathing) and the pulse races. Changes in posture,

for example on sitting from lying down, cause the pulse to rise and a feeling of faintness.

Swelling:
peripheral oedema makes the face puffy with bags under the eyes, rings on fingers feel tight and ankles show the imprint of stocking elastic. Swelling is worst in the morning and wears off after rising.

Act: rest, wait and see. Do not give oxygen because it may fool you into thinking the victim is better. If he has not improved within 24 hours consider he has severe AMS, and descend.

Mild AMS may blend unnoticed into severe AMS. HACO or HAPO become manifest depending on whether body water settles in the brain or the lungs or both. The amount of peripheral oedema indicates the severity of AMS, so it is better to make a mistake by diagnosing the condition as severe AMS and to descend, than to underestimate mild AMS. The entire drama can unfold within hours and usually does so at night.

Severe AMS

HIGH ALTITUDE CEREBRAL OEDEMA (HACO)
HACO is like an exaggerated form of mild AMS and usually occurs above 4,000m (c13,000ft); although less common than HAPO, 60% of victims will have HAPO as well. Symptoms of HACO and HAPO may overlap so it is difficult to tell which is which. Severe AMS can kill quickly, so make a confident diagnosis and act decisively.

Headache:
severe, constant and throbbing like a bad toothache or migraine. No relief comes from paracetamol (D.1.1), codeine (D.1.3), a night's sleep or massaging the temples.

Inco-ordination (ataxia):
the victim staggers as if drunk, and fumbles fine movements
such as handling a camera. To distinguish ataxia from simple
tiredness make him perform the following tasks and compare with a normal person as a control:
   – Toe-to-heel walking: place the heel of one foot against the
toes of the other and walk along a 4m straight line drawn in
the snow or on the ground. An ataxic person will sway, stag-
ger and fall over when told to turn round and walk back.
   – Sitting upright without support: a person with ataxia of
the trunk will roll over.

Languor:
extreme fatigue is not reversed by rest. Pressure on the brain
blunts the intellect. The victim won't talk, eat or drink; he
lies curled up in a sleeping bag avoiding contact with the
outside world; he is apathetic and isolated, yet irritable and
confused. If still active, he may show poor judgement and
thus make bad mountaineering decisions. Sleep is fitful and
punctuated by bad dreams. He may hallucinate, hear voices,
or see non-existent companions. He may be incontinent.
   N.B. Both ataxia and languor are common to hypothermia
(take the rectal temperature), alcohol intoxication (smell the
breath) and opiate drug abuse (look for pin-point pupils).

Vomiting:
severe vomiting leads to dehydration which cannot be
reversed by drinking. Urine is scanty and dark yellow.

   Eye signs: swelling of the optic nerve head (papilloedema), only
   visible with an ophthalmoscope by a skilled observer, signifies
   raised (intracranial) pressure within the skull and brain.

Coma:
finally the drowsy victim becomes unrousable, drifts into

coma and may die. Convulsions are rare. Cerebral oedema victims can remain unconscious for days and yet recover completely.

HIGH ALTITUDE RETINAL HAEMORRHAGE (HARH)

One third of all climbers going very high (above 6,000m/c20,000ft) have haemorrhages in the retina at the back of the eye. The diagnosis requires an ophthalmoscope.

The haemorrhages look like red paint splashed on a wall. Usually they cause no symptoms, however, if the sensitive macula area, which interprets fine vision like reading, is involved a blurred or blank patch may be present in the central vision. These retinal haemorrhages heal in a few weeks and usually leave no scars, but if present in the brain they may be more harmful.

HIGH ALTITUDE PULMONARY OEDEMA (HAPO)

In HAPO the lungs become waterlogged, hindering the passage of oxygen into the blood. So the victim can drown in his own juices.

HAPO is rare below 3,000m (c10,000ft); it begins 36 to 72 hours after arriving at altitude and is cured by descent. Rest and oxygen may help temporarily. It affects children more than adults, men and women equally. It may be related to severe exertion and rate of climb. It worsens at night when oxygen saturation is low owing to the quiet breathing of sleep and to periodic Cheyne-Stokes breathing, which is exaggerated in HAPO. Those who have gone too high for their own good and have suffered HAPO before may suffer again and at a similar altitude.

SIGNS OF HAPO

Shortness of breath (dyspnoea):
occurs on slight exertion and is even present at rest. Breath-

ing is irregular and fast at more than 25 breaths per minute. The victim does not improve with rest, and is hungry for air. The chest feels full and tight, but there is no actual pain, which distinguishes it from heart attack or pneumonia.

Cough and sputum:
early cough is tickling, hacking, and dry – without sputum. Later the sputum is frothy because of air bubbling through oedema fluid in the alveoli, and pink and blood flecked because of capillary blood leaks. By contrast sputum in pneumonia or bronchitis is yellow-green owing to pus in the alveoli, and fever is present.

Chest sounds:
crackling, moist sounds (crepitations), like rubbing hair between finger and thumb beside the ear, can be heard with a stethoscope or by placing an ear against the back of the victim. The noise is due to air bubbling through fluid and can make a clearly audible rattling sound in both lungs, or on one side alone.

Cyanosis:
at rest the lips, face and finger-nails look blue in natural light because haemoglobin is less saturated with oxygen than normal. A coloured tent will obscure cyanosis.

Pulse:
the pulse will be rapid, more than 110 beats per minute.

Act: *descent* usually cures severe AMS miraculously. Do not delay because of night, inconvenience, experimenting with drugs or oxygen, or in expectation of a mountain rescue team or helicopter – unless descending through difficult terrain in the dark will endanger the whole party. The victim, always accompanied and perhaps carried, should descend at least 300m, preferably 1,000m. Even a modest descent can save life. The greater and faster the descent, the more swift the recovery. Once down the victim should stay down until he can be examined by a wise physician.

The forms of treatment listed below play for time but should never take preference over evacuating the victim immediately to a lower altitude. He may just want to lie in bed, sniff oxygen and drink tea; but he needs to *descend*, if necessary by compulsion.

Rest:
prop the victim up, so oedema fluid sinks to the bottom of his lungs and pools in his legs. Cold and anxiety aggravate AMS, so keep him warm and relaxed.

Oxygen:
100% oxygen flowing at 6 litres per minute given via a tight-fitting mask is optimal, but settle for less if the supply is meagre. A change in the victim's colour from blue to pink shows the effectiveness of oxygen which may relieve head-ache and help pulmonary oedema; but it is merely an adjunct to, not a substitute for, descent.

Fluids:
drink (4 to 5 litres daily minimum) enough to maintain a copious flow of urine (1 litre daily minimum).

Drugs:
relying on drugs to permit rapid ascent is idiotic. However acetazolamide and dexamethasone taken in small doses reduce significantly the chance of getting AMS and the severity should it occur.

Treat: *acetazolamide* (Diamox): (D.6.2) 125–250mg twice daily, a mild diuretic that appears to help acclimatization without masking the symptoms of AMS (unlike steroids), and diminishes the incidence and severity of AMS symptoms of headache or nausea. It prevents or reduces AMS symptoms in people such as rescuers, who have to ascend hurriedly to altitude, if taken on the day of arrival at altitude and for 3 days after. It diminishes Cheyne-Stokes breathing and thereby improves the quality of sleep and maintains oxygenation in the newly arrived at altitude. Symptoms of tingling hands and feet (and a foul taste to beer) can be ignored. Do not give Diamox to someone with a known allergy to sulpha drugs.

dexamethasone (Decadron) (D.4.2): 4mg twice daily starting on the day of ascent and for 3 to 5 days thereafter for preventing AMS; for treating it, 10mg i/v then 4mg every 6 hours. It is a powerful steroid used in neurosurgery to shrink the brain, hence its beneficial effect in AMS and HACO. But never use it with the aim of allowing further ascent.

morphine (D.1.4): a powerful analgesic useful in a person with severe headache and ataxia; it allays the crippling anxiety of HAPO. Morphine dilates peripheral blood vessels so blood is shifted away from the lungs thereby easing HAPO. It depresses breathing so never use it in HACO, and be cautious in HAPO. It has no effect on acclimatization.

other drugs: digitalis is useless in HAPO as the victim is not in heart failure. Frusemide (Lasix), once popular, is now discredited. Antibiotics only help in the presence of chest infection – with fever, pussy spit and crepitations. Spironolactone and antacids are unproven.

Gamow bag – a portable, (but heavy and bulky) inflatable pressure chamber can lower the virtual atmospheric pressure while the person is in the bag. Its effect can be dramatic. Tourniquets and intermittent positive pressure breathing have no place in the outdoors.

With good sense Acute Mountain Sickness and its sinister offspring, High Altitude Cerebral and Pulmonary Oedema, should not happen. But if they do, prevent their deadly consequences, by rapid descent to a lower altitude.

22

IMMUNIZATION

N.B. Most of the specialized drugs mentioned in this chapter do not appear in the general drugs section on page 27 and are not enclosed in square brackets.

Travellers to tropical and subtropical countries can be protected by immunization against certain infectious diseases. Inoculation with a small amount of the disease-causing organism, or a purified derivative of its toxin, produces immune antibodies which protect against attacking organisms or their toxins.

Some vaccines require several doses spaced apart, therefore plan an immunization schedule 3 months ahead of your intended departure. In emergency a crash course can be given in 15 days. The local public health departments will have up-to-date information on international immunization requirements.

Anyone suffering from immuno-suppression, eczema or severe allergy, pregnant women or those taking steroid medication (cortisone or prednisone) should avoid immunization. If wishing to travel, they need a certificate of exemption from their doctor.

Unexplained fever developing in the tropics, or soon after return therefrom, warrants consultation with a doctor who can carry out screening, preferably one with knowledge of, or access to information, about tropical diseases.

Ideal schedule week	1	2	3	4	5	6	7	8	9
Diphtheria/ tetanus		x							
Typhoid	x				x		x (optional)		
Cholera		x			x		x		
Polio	x								
Yellow Fever				x					
I.S.G.								x	

Crash course days	1	5	12	15
Diphtheria/ tetanus		x		
Typhoid		x	x	x
Cholera	x		x	x
Polio		x		
Yellow Fever	x			
I.S.G.			x	

Immunizations to be considered

TETANUS AND DIPHTHERIA

These diseases are often fatal. Immunization gives complete protection; a sore, stiff arm and headache that lasts a couple of days is a small price to pay. Tetanus (lockjaw) still occurs in Britain and North America, although it is more common abroad.

Most people in Western countries are immunized against tetanus and diphtheria in early childhood; in the rare case of an adult who escaped, primary immunization can be obtained by 2 i/m injections spaced 8 weeks apart. Protection lasts for 10 years then you need a booster dose DT/Vac/Ads (Adult) 0.5ml i/m. After a dirty wound or an animal bite get a booster dose if you have had an immunization within the last 5 years, or if in any doubt about being up-to-date with your shots.

Act: clean wounds thoroughly because tetanus spores lie dormant in the soil where horse and sheep manure abounds. Tetanus should be treated in hospital with human tetanus immune globulin 3–10,000 U i/m, and penicillin 1,000,000 U every 4 hours or tetracycline 500mg every 6 hours, each for 5 days.

TYPHOID AND PARATYPHOID

If travelling to the tropics where typhoid is endemic, have a single booster dose – Typhim Vi 0.5ml s/c or i/m – a vaccine prepared from killed bacteria which offers reasonable protection for 3 years. The injection may cause local soreness, headache, fever and malaise for a couple of days, during which time avoid alcohol.

A new oral typhoid vaccine – Vivotif 3 capsules on alternate days – has fewer adverse effects, but less protection (1 year). Scrupulous hygiene with water, food and toilet is the only safeguard.

CHOLERA

Immunization is not recommended for tourists because the risk of cholera to them is low and the vaccine is poorly effective. Some countries (public health authorities should know which) demand a single dose for travellers from an infected area. The international certificate is valid for 6 months only.

POLIOMYELITIS

Immunization is given to most schoolchildren and lasts a lifetime; it consists of 3 doses of live trivalent oral polio vaccine (OPV), or 4 doses of inactivated polio vaccine (IPV), with an IPV booster every 5 years until age 18. If travelling in places with an increased risk of polio, such as living rough where sanitation is poor (polio virus is carried in faeces), anyone under 40 needs a single booster dose of Pol/Vac (oral) 3 drops. Protection from polio is painless; the paralysing disease is deadly.

HEPATITIS A

Hepatitis A virus is carried in faeces and acquired from infected food and water, or by swimming near a sewage outlet. It is a common, miserable disease that can be fatal, but it is completely preventable. Jaundice follows 3 to 7 days of vague, unpleasant malaise. Rest is the only treatment.

For a visit of less than 4 months, immune serum globulin (ISG) is useful protection against hepatitis A – 1ml for every month of travel, plus 1ml extra for good measure. Protection is good for 4 months, only partial for a further 2 months; repeat it if the danger of infection persists. ISG interferes with antibody formation, so have it last after all the other immunizations.

For a longer visit, Havrix 1 dose 3 weeks before departure and a booster after 6 months gives cover for 10 years.

HEPATITIS B

Hepatitis B vaccine is recommended for travellers to highly endemic areas like South-east Asia and sub-Saharan Africa, those likely to come in contact with blood or secretions of potentially infected persons, or those on a sexual spree. Chance infection is most unlikely. Hep B is even more serious than Hep A, causing chronic liver disease.

Treat: 3 doses of vaccine needed: first at elected date; second 1 month later; third – if you are in a hurry – can be 2 months after second dose with a booster at 12 months, otherwise third dose at 6 months. It should be administered intra-muscularly into deltoid or thigh but not buttock muscle. 0–12 year olds need 10mcgs (0.5 ml), adults need 20mcg (1.0 ml).

TUBERCULOSIS

BCG immunization is given only to high risk travellers such as medical personnel who have a negative tuberculin (Mantoux) skin test.

MEASLES

Anyone born after 1956 who has not had measles, or who has not had the vaccine, should receive a single 1ml dose.

YELLOW FEVER

Yellow fever used to be a common killer but is now quite rare. It is carried by mosquitos from mammals, principally monkeys, to man.

Immunization is advisable before travelling to infected areas (the forests of Central and South America, and East, Central and West Africa); some countries demand vaccination for travellers from these areas. The live virus vaccine can be obtained from officially designated centres, and the dose is 0.5ml by s/c injection. An International Certificate is valid for 10 days after immunization and lasts for 10 years.

SMALLPOX

Vaccination should no longer be given because smallpox has been eradicated worldwide. But a few countries still insist on a valid International Certificate showing vaccination within the previous 3 years.

RABIES

Modern rabies vaccine is highly purified, safe and effective, but very expensive. In view of the cost and the low risk to normal travellers, immunization is only recommended for those anticipating contact with rabies-bearing animals, or those going into an area where rabies is a constant threat. Instead carry the vaccine in a kit and only give it if bitten or licked by a rabid creature.

MENINGITIS (meningococcal)

Occurs rarely in outbreaks and may be fatal. Immunization with a single injection lasts 3 years or more and is free of side-effects.

MALARIA

No immunization is available against malaria which is caused by the mosquito-borne parasites, Plasmodium falciparum, P. vivax, P. malariae and P. ovale. Chloroquine-resistant P. falciparum has become a potentially deadly problem for travellers worldwide – so consult a specialist travel clinic or health centre before you go. In the UK advice is available from the Hospital for Tropical Diseases Healthline (Tel: 0839 337733) or the London School of Hygiene & Tropical Medicine Healthline (Tel: 0891 600350); in the USA from the Centre for Disease Control http:/www.cdc.gov/travel/travel.html.

Prevention:
no immunization is available so the best protection is
common sense. Anti-malarial drugs only suppress the parasite; they must be taken regularly to maintain an adequate
blood concentration, are not 100% effective, and often have
unpleasant adverse effects.

Almost nowhere is chloroquine alone an adequate prevention. Travellers to chloroquine-resistant areas should take
Mefloquine 250mg once weekly or Chloroquine (300mg
base) weekly plus Proguanil 200mg daily (available to UK
travellers), depending on the level of drug-resistance in the
area to be visited. Mefloquine offers the greatest protection
in most areas but unpleasant neuro-psychiatric adverse
effects may occur, and its suitability should be discussed
with a health professional well in advance of the trip.

Mosquitos tend to bite around dusk, but are discouraged
by long sleeves, trousers, insect repellent and by mosquito
netting over beds. It only takes one bite from an infected
mosquito to pass on malaria, so there is risk even on a brief
stop-over in a malarial area.

Symptoms of malaria:
an attack is heralded by a mild fever and sore muscles,
followed over several days by chills and high fever. The
victim can shiver so violently the bed shakes, teeth chatter,
the skin becomes blue and cold and the pulse races. An hour
later the person becomes hot with a temperature up to 41°C
(107°F), is flushed, suffers severe headache and may be
delirious. Then the temperature falls, profuse sweating
occurs and the person begins to feel better again. This cycle
repeats, usually over several days, and in the case of the
most dangerous species of malaria can give rise to serious
complications and sometimes death. The parasite can be seen
under the microscope.

Act: seek medical advice urgently to establish a diagnosis.

A diagnosis of malaria can be confirmed using either a blood film or recently marketed commercial kits (for the diagnosis of P.falciparum malaria) which are available in some countries including the UK.

Start treatment immediately if you cannot reach medical help. In chloroquine-resistant areas take a course of quinine (600mg (2 tablets) 3 times daily for 5 days, or until 24 hours after the fever has subsided). Follow with a single dose of 3 tablets of Fansidar (25mg pyrimethamine + 500mg sulphadoxine), or a course of doxycycline one 100mg tablet twice daily for 7 days.

INDEX

THE MOUNTAINEERS, founded in 1906, is a nonprofit outdoor activity and conservation club, whose mission is "to explore, study, preserve, and enjoy the natural beauty of the outdoors. . . . " Based in Seattle, Washington, the club is now the third-largest such organization in the United States, with 15,000 members and five branches throughout Washington State.

The Mountaineers sponsors both classes and year-round outdoor activities in the Pacific Northwest, which include hiking, mountain climbing, ski-touring, snowshoeing, bicycling, camping, kayaking and canoeing, nature study, sailing, and adventure travel. The club's conservation division supports environmental causes through educational activities, sponsoring legislation, and presenting informational programs. All club activities are led by skilled, experienced volunteers, who are dedicated to promoting safe and responsible enjoyment and preservation of the outdoors.

If you would like to participate in these organized outdoor activities or the club's programs, consider a membership in The Mountaineers. For information and an application, write or call The Mountaineers, Club Headquarters, 300 Third Avenue West, Seattle, Washington 98119, (206) 284-6310.

The Mountaineers Books, an active, nonprofit publishing program of the club, produces guidebooks, instructional texts, historical works, natural history guides, and works on environmental conservation. All books produced by The Mountaineers are aimed at fulfilling the club's mission.

Send or call for our catalog of more than 300 outdoor titles:

The Mountaineers Books
1001 SW Klickitat Way, Suite 201
Seattle, WA 98134
1-800-553-4453
mbooks@mountaineers.org
www.mountaineers.org

WILDERNESS NAVIGATION: Finding Your Way Using Map, Compass, Altimeter, and GPS
Bob Burns and Mike Burns
Complete guide to navigating on- and off-trail in the backcountry, with 30 practice problems and up-to-date declination maps.

WILDERNESS 911: A Step-by-Step Guide for Medical Emergencies and Improvised Care in the Backcountry
Eric Weiss, M.D.
Quick-access wilderness medicine from *BACKPACKER* magazine experts.

MOUNTAINEERING: The Freedom of the Hills
The Mountaineers; Don Graydon and Kurt Hanson, Editors
Completely revised and expanded edition of the classic text on climbing and mountaineering techniques.

BACKPACKER'S EVERYDAY WISDOM: 1001 Expert Tips for Hikers, *Karen Berger*
Expert tips and tricks for hikers and backpackers selected from one of the most popular *BACKPACKER* magazine columns.

WILDERNESS BASICS: The Complete Handbook for Hikers & Backpackers, 2nd Edition
Jerry Schad and David Moser, Editors
Covers backcountry use from planning and equipment to weather and first aid.

AVALANCHE SAFETY FOR SKIERS AND CLIMBERS, 2nd Edition, *Tony Daffern*
Thoroughly illustrated manual on avoidance of avalanche hazard by good routefinding and recognition of dangerous slopes.

BACKPACKER'S BACKCOUNTRY COOKING: From Pack to Plate in 10 Minutes, *Dorcas Miller*
Over 144 recipes and trailtested advice on how to plan and pack simple meals, selected from the *BACKPACKER* magazine column.